Heather Butler has taught at primary l
particular emphasis on special needs, ar
teaching and nurturing of children withi
years. She now teaches part-time in a prim
and leads INSET training, as well as RE a
writing workshops in primary schools across the UK. Heather has been involved with several charities caring for traumatised children across the world and is author of over 30 books for children and teachers, including 35 Stories to Make You Think *(Barnabas, 2008). Find out more about Heather by visiting her website at www.heatherbutler.info.*

Published by
The Bible Reading Fellowship
15 The Chambers, Vineyard
Abingdon OX14 3FE
United Kingdom
Tel: +44 (0)1865 319700
Email: enquiries@brf.org.uk
Website: www.brf.org.uk
BRF is a Registered Charity

ISBN 978 1 84101 703 7
First published 2011
10 9 8 7 6 5 4 3 2 1 0

Acknowledgments
Unless otherwise stated, scripture quotations are taken from the Contemporary English Version of the Bible published by HarperCollins Publishers, copyright © 1991, 1992, 1995 American Bible Society.

A catalogue record for this book is available from the British Library

Printed in Singapore by Craft Print International Ltd

Story Assemblies of 24 Saints

24 off-the-peg assembly plans for the school year

Heather Butler

With thanks to the children and staff at Manor Farm Community Junior School, Hazlemere, Buckinghamshire, who let me try ideas out on them.

Photocopy permission

The Copyright Licensing Agency (CLA)

BRF is a Registered Charity (No. 233280)

Contents

+

Foreword

I first worked with Heather over five years ago when she came to teach RE to all the children in my school. She did this with creativity and enthusiasm in her own inimitable manner, thereby inspiring the children to learn through a diverse range of styles.

Heather has also been into school on several occasions to deliver her creative writing days. Laden with props, from pirate ships to puppets, she has a knack for drawing children in to a wonderful world where they are enabled to allow their own imagination to run riot. The result of this has been children's writing of a very high standard, including from those who have not previously viewed themselves as 'writers' and for whom writing had meant a real challenge that they may or may not have overcome.

One of the greatest assets of Heather's latest book of assembly resources is that it is written not only by a great storyteller but by one with a teacher's perspective. This means that you will not need to spend hours preparing the assembly or gathering resources. As every busy teacher knows, that means a great deal.

Each one of the 24 story assemblies is presented in the same way and you can choose to simply tell the story or to make it interactive. The background to each saint is succinctly given, so you will quickly gain an understanding yourself if the subject is new to you. When I have used Heather's assemblies in school, the children have been fully engaged with the message being conveyed, the characters in the story and the humour. It's not easy to think of new ideas to keep the whole school interested. Well, now we don't have to; Heather has done it for us!

Sue Harratt
Head teacher, Woodside Junior School, Amersham, Bucks

+

Introduction

Story Assemblies of 24 Saints contains 24 complete assembly plans ready for teachers to pick off the shelf and deliver as a whole-school, year-group or classroom assembly. The material is designed to meet the needs of busy teachers looking for flexible and creative material to take them through the school year. Each assembly plan includes a creative mix of elements, designed to put the life of the featured saint in context and, through storytelling and focused reflection, help children think about what the message of the saint's story might mean to their own lives today. A suggestion for a relevant symbol is provided with each story, designed to highlight a special feature about the saint and help children use their imaginations to ground the story.

The 24 saints' days are spread across the school year from September to July, so teachers can opt in at any time. Each assembly provides:

- Teacher's notes, giving background details and essential information to help set the scene and ensure that the teacher has everything to hand for the smooth running of the assembly. Information includes:
    - Theme: A short phrase to instantly identify what the assembly is about.
    - Bible link: Helpful Bible verses written out in full, with a short commentary about how the Bible story fits into the theme of the storytelling.
    - Resources: Suggestions for visual aids and props to help bring the story to life during the storytelling.
    - Saint in context: Background information to place the saint in the context of his or her culture and time.

- ❖ Entry point: Topical introduction to the theme of the story and questions to help children see how the theme is relevant to their own lives.
- ❖ Reflection: Imaginative guide to help children reflect on the story and what its message might mean for them.
- ❖ Suggested songs: Songs that reflect the theme of the assembly.
- ❖ Optional prayer: Suggestions for a Christian prayer, picking out the main themes of the story.
- ❖ 'Build a saint' activity: Classroom follow-up to help build a full picture of the saint, explore a symbol to help children remember how he or she is traditionally recognised, and create a classroom display. In general, the activities use simple, readily available objects, drawing and colouring materials, air-dry modelling clay or play dough.

- The story, offering a choice of two storytelling methods: a simple retelling, ideal for younger children, and an interactive questioning alternative for older children. Many of the interactive options also include ideas for children to act out the story as it unfolds.

+

— 16 September —

Ninian

Teacher's notes

Theme

This assembly is about who guides us.

Bible link

I am the good shepherd, and the good shepherd gives up his life for his sheep.
JOHN 10:11

Jesus described himself as a shepherd who knows and looks after his sheep. We read in the Bible that Jesus said he would even die for his sheep, which Christians believe he did at Easter time. The story of Ninian is a story about a shepherd in the Christian tradition.

Resources

A toy sheep, a container for soup such as a flask or bottle, a walking stick or shepherd's crook, a blanket for the elderly man

Saint in context

Traditionally, it is thought that Ninian was born in Cumbria and went to Rome as a young man to study Christianity. He was made a bishop and returned to Britain around AD397. After building a stone church in Whithorn, south-west Scotland, he began converting the Picts to Christianity. Ninian, whose Scottish name is Saint Ringan, is first mentioned by the historian Bede (AD673–735).

Entry point

Talk about how large ships are guided into harbour by small tug boats. Alternatively, talk about how dogs help guide people who have difficulty seeing.

Everyone needs to be guided. Ask the children to think of someone who has guided them recently. Share how the children were helped, and by whom.

Reflection

Talk about people who help and guide us. For example, people give us guidance about eating the right foods, crossing the road safely and knowing how to look after our pets. Invite the children to think of someone who guided them and helped them to find something... learn something... avoid getting something wrong... go somewhere. Who guides us the most? Does anyone ever guide us to do things we know are wrong?

Suggested songs

- Give me oil in my lamp, keep me burning (*Come and Praise* 43)
- If I go to the furthest place (*Songs for Every Assembly*, Out of the Ark Music)

Optional prayer

Dear God, thank you for being like a shepherd who cares and wants the best for his sheep. Thank you that when we ask, you will help us to make good decisions and will guide us.

'Build a saint' activity

Use pipe cleaners and cotton wool to make fluffy sheep. Add the sheep to a classroom display as a symbol to remind children about the story of Ninian and the shepherd boy. Jesus described himself as the 'good shepherd' and his followers as sheep. Draw a sheepfold with a shepherd guarding and guiding his flock. The drawings can also be added to the display.

The story retold

NB: This story happened a long time ago. People shared what they had, and shepherd boys were usually teenagers.

A shepherd boy worked on a hillside, looking after sheep, making sure his sheep were safe and had enough food to eat. Each evening he counted them as they passed into the sheepfold where they spent the night. He would see the short sheep (their tummies scratched across the grass when they walked), the shooting-up sheep (they seemed to grow taller every day) and the shabby sheep that needed a wash. He knew each of them by name.

Tonight was Christmas Eve and the boy was keen to return home as early as possible. He herded the sheep back to the fold and counted them as they went in. He was one short sheep short.

What a nuisance—and tonight of all nights, when his family would be waiting for him! As quickly as he could, he set off back to the hills to look for the short sheep that was missing, taking with him some soup in case he became hungry.

Well, that short sheep was nowhere to be found. Absolutely nowhere! The shepherd boy looked in the fields, behind rocks, under trees, down holes, beneath bushes and over hills. But he was still a short sheep short.

'Short sheep, where are you?' he sighed. 'It's Christmas

Eve and I need someone to show me where to look.' He sat for a while, wondering what to do, pouring himself some soup while he thought, then pausing as he heard footsteps behind him.

'You'll find the sheep over there,' an elderly man said, pointing into the next field. The boy was more than surprised. What was an elderly man doing on the hills at this time of night, and how had he known why the boy was there?

The shepherd boy offered the elderly man some of his soup and they sat together, drinking it.

'I'm on my way to Bethlehem,' the elderly man told him. 'Something special is happening there tonight and I don't want to miss out on it.'

Bethlehem! That was miles away.

'I must be on my way,' the man said, 'and you must go and find your sheep.' With that, he stood up and walked on.

The boy, too, stood up and went to the field the elderly man had pointed to. There was his woolly friend, waiting for him.

'I'm not a short sheep short any more!' the shepherd boy laughed. 'Now let's hurry up, because my family will be waiting for me.'

No one knows for sure, but tradition has it that even though he had died many years before, the elderly man was St Ninian—doing what he had done when he was alive, helping others and guiding them whenever he could.

Interactive retelling

Choose a child to be the shepherd boy and act out the story as it unfolds.

Story: A young shepherd boy is on the hillside, looking after his sheep. It is Christmas Eve and he is looking forward to going home early to be with his family.

Interactive question: What would it be like to be a shepherd boy?

Story: At the end of the day, he counts the sheep's legs and divides the number by four. (He doesn't actually do this, but he does count the sheep.)

Action: Ask several children to be sheep and supervise them being counted.

Story: That night, the shepherd boy is one sheep short—one short sheep short. The tall sheep are all here. So are the shabby sheep. It is a short sheep he is missing. 'Surely I'm not one short sheep short,' he shivers. The shepherd boy counts again. He is still one short sheep short.

Interactive questions: What are his options now? What would you do? Why?

Story: The shepherd boy cares about his sheep. So he makes sure the other sheep are safe, then sets off, back to where the sheep have spent their day on the hillside.

He takes some soup with him in case he becomes hungry. He looks in the fields, behind rocks, under trees, down holes, beneath bushes, over hills. Is that short sheep anywhere to be found? Of course he isn't. The boy sits down and sighs. 'I need someone to help me and tell me what to do,' he says. He slowly begins pouring out some of his soup.

Interactive question: What could happen next?

Story: As he begins to drink his soup, there is a rustling behind him, but it isn't the short sheep. No. It's an elderly man, who begins chatting to the boy.

Action: Choose a child to be the elderly man and sit next to the shepherd boy drinking soup.

Story: The shepherd boy offers the elderly man some soup and they sit together, drinking it. 'I'm on my way to Bethlehem,' the man tells the boy. 'Something special is happening there tonight and I don't want to miss out on it.' Bethlehem! That is miles away, the boy thinks. A short while later, the elderly man says, 'I must be on my way… and the sheep you are looking for is in the field over there.' With that, he stands up and walks on. The boy checks out where the man had said and there is his short sheep's shadow, shamelessly shivering in the cold damp night. The boy picks up the short sheep and heads for home.

No one knows for sure, but tradition has it that, even though he had died many years before, the elderly man was St Ninian—doing what he had done when he was alive, helping others and guiding them whenever he could.

Interactive question: Imagine you were the shepherd boy, telling your parents or friends about what had happened. What would you say to them?

+

— 21 September —

Matthew

Teacher's notes

Theme

This assembly is about what we are good at.

Bible link

As Jesus was leaving, he saw a tax collector named Matthew sitting at the place for paying taxes. Jesus said to him, 'Come with me.' Matthew got up and went with him.
MATTHEW 9:9

It was probably Matthew the tax collector who wrote one of the Gospels about Jesus. Matthew's Gospel uses Old Testament references to God's chosen king—the Messiah—to anchor his record of who he believes Jesus is. Along with Matthew, Christians believe that God's chosen Messiah is Jesus. Jesus invited Matthew to join him as one of his band of followers. The tax collector's encounter with Jesus that day completely changed his life.

Resources

Simple robes for Matthew to wear, a table for him to sit behind, a pile of coins

Saint in context

As a tax collector, Matthew would have been able to read and write, but he worked for the occupying Roman forces, which was not a popular job option. His income would probably have been supplemented by money gained by overcharging people, so he would have been doubly unpopular. Matthew is sometimes called Levi, although the name Matthew is more commonly used once he becomes a follower of Jesus. Matthew grew up in Galilee, but it is thought that he might have been born in Syria. He was one of the disciples involved in establishing the Christian Church after Jesus' death and resurrection.

Entry point

Invite the children to tell everyone what their friends and other children in their classes are good at. Extend the question to include what the school is good at, and celebrate musical, sports and any other recent achievements.

Reflection

Matthew is thought to have used his writing skills to record what Jesus did while he was alive. Talk about things we are good at, including qualities such as being kind, looking out for other people, playing well in a team, making other people laugh and so on. How can we use one thing we are good at today to help someone else?

Suggested songs

- He made me (*Come and Praise* 18)
- If I had a hammer (*Come and Praise* 71)
- Praise the Lord in everything (*Come and Praise* 33)
- Life is a wonderful thing (*Songs for Every Assembly*, Out of the Ark Music)

Optional prayer

Dear God, thank you for the gifts you have given us. Help us to use them today to help other people.

'Build a saint' activity

Matthew's Gospel tells the story of Jesus' birth and the visit of the wise men. Make a paper crown as a symbol to remind the children of the story of Matthew. The crown can also represent Jesus—God's chosen king—or the wise men who came to worship him after he was born.

The story retold

Matthew was a tax collector—an unpopular, dishonest, sad, scheming, cheating, low-grade tax collector who worked for the occupying Roman forces. Matthew spent all day collecting money from people. When fishermen caught a few fish, they had to pay tax. When bees produced honey, beekeepers had to pay tax. When a carpenter sold a table, he had to pay tax. When a farmer bought a new ox to pull his plough, he had to pay tax. Everyone complained because they paid too much tax.

Matthew could read and write and was good with numbers. In his day, not everyone could do that. Matthew could have chosen to teach other people how to read and write: he could have worked in the school at the synagogue. But he didn't. Instead, he sat behind a table and collected money, which he stacked into piles of shiny coins. Matthew continually counted and checked the growing piles of coins and, when he became bored, he checked them again. Sometimes he overcharged people and put some of the coins in his own pocket.

One day, as Matthew dribbled and drooled over the coins he had collected and thought about how very clever he was, someone walked by. This person didn't have any taxes to pay. He simply stopped in front of Matthew's table and invited him to leave the tax collecting and join him.

Matthew looked up at the person standing in front of him. Travelling preachers often passed by but there was something different about this man. Without hesitation, Matthew stood up, left his job as a tax collector and went with Jesus.

Some of Jesus' other friends might not have been too impressed. They would probably have given Matthew money in order to pay their taxes, and they would have known how dishonest he was. But the fact that Matthew was a tax collector didn't bother Jesus. Perhaps he knew that one day Matthew would be able to use what he was good at to help others. It is thought that Matthew the tax collector, who was good with numbers and could read and write, later used his talents to write about Jesus' life, and that the first book in the New Testament, known as Matthew's Gospel, is named after him because he wrote it.

Interactive retelling

Dress a child up to be Matthew and sit him or her behind a table while others come and pay their taxes, complaining as they walk away from the table.

Story: Matthew is a tax collector—an unpopular, dishonest, unpatriotic, sad, scheming, cheating, low-grade tax collector who works for the occupying Roman forces.

He spends all day collecting money from people. When fishermen catch a few fish, they have to pay tax. When bees produce honey, the beekeepers have to pay tax. When a carpenter sells a table, he has to pay tax. When a farmer buys a new ox to pull his plough, he has to pay tax. Everyone complains because they pay too much tax.

Interactive question: The taxes are collected by the occupying Roman forces. What are they used for?

Action: Ask the child playing Matthew to mime, with clear facial expressions, while the following lines are read.

Story: Matthew can read and write and is good with numbers. He sits behind a table collecting money, which he stacks into piles of shiny coins. Matthew continually counts and checks the growing piles of coins and, when he becomes bored, he checks them again. Sometimes he overcharges people and puts some of the coins in his own pocket.

Action: Choose a child to play Jesus and act out the following paragraph, with Matthew behind his table and Jesus walking towards him.

Story: One day, as Matthew dribbles and drools over the money he has collected, and stacks and checks and rechecks, and thinks how very clever he is, someone walks by. This person doesn't have any taxes to pay, so he does not complain to Matthew. He simply stops in front of the table and invites Matthew to leave the tax collecting and join him.

Interactive question: What might have been the first response to come into Matthew's mind?

Action: Act out the following paragraph with Matthew and Jesus.

Story: Matthew looks up at the person standing in front of him. Travelling preachers often pass by but there is something different about this man. Without hesitation, Matthew stands up, leaves his job as a tax collector and follows Jesus.

Interactive question: Why might some of Jesus' other friends not be too impressed with Jesus' choice of Matthew as a friend?

Story: The fact that Matthew is a tax collector doesn't bother Jesus. Perhaps he knows that one day Matthew will be able to use what he is good at to help others. People think that Matthew the tax collector, who was good with numbers and could read and write, later used his talents to write about Jesus' life, and that the first book in the New Testament, known as Matthew's Gospel, is named after him because he wrote it.

+

— 30 September —

Jerome

Teacher's notes

This assembly is about being friends.

Bible link

Leopards will lie down with young goats, and wolves will rest with lambs. Calves and lions will eat together and be cared for by little children.

ISAIAH 11:6

The Bible talks about people getting along with each other and being friends. The prophet Isaiah writes about wolves and sheep living together in peace, calves and lion cubs feeding together and little children taking care of them. Traditional stories about Jerome being accompanied by a lion reflect this idea.

Resources

A mask or name label for the lion, donkey and camels, striped T-shirts for the robbers, blankets for the monks, Hebrew and Latin writing downloaded from the internet (optional)

Saint in context

Jerome was born about AD347 in Stridon, Dalmatia. His parents were rich and he was well educated and well travelled, especially in France and Italy. Jerome had a bad temper and didn't always get on very well with other people. Jerome lived in Bethlehem for many years, built a monastery there and lived as a monk. By the time he died in 420, he had translated the Old Testament from Hebrew to

Latin, the language used for writing in Europe at the time. Through his work, many more people were able to read the Bible.

Entry point

Talk with the children about the things that help us most of all to get along with other people and to be friends. What prevents us from getting along with others?

Reflection

Talk about the people and animals in the story who spoke to each other in a friendly way. Who do we find it difficult to get on with, and why? When might we have a chance to do something with that person that would help us to get along together? Is there a difference between being friends with someone and just 'getting along'?

Suggested songs

- O Lord, all the world belongs to you (*Come and Praise* 39)
- The building song (*Come and Praise* 61)
- Peace is flowing (*Come and Praise* 144)

Optional prayer

Dear God, it's really hard sometimes to get on and live in peace with everyone. Help us today to try extra hard to include everyone in our games so that no one is left out, and to work together as teams.

'Build a saint' activity

Add a cuddly toy lion to the classroom display table as a symbol to remind the children about the story of Jerome. Ask the children to draw pictures of lions doing unlikely things, such as cooking with a chef or talking to a gerbil, as a reminder of the promise that in God's kingdom everyone will live in peace.

The story retold

Jerome lived about 1600 years ago, which is a very, very long time ago. In his day, the Bible was mostly written in a language called Hebrew. Jerome was one of the few people who could read Hebrew. He had the idea of writing the Bible in a language that many people of his day could read. Because Jerome could read Hebrew, he was able to translate the Bible into Latin, which he could also understand. Thanks to Jerome, many people were then able to read and understand what it said. He did his translation work while he was living as a monk in a monastery in Bethlehem, the town where Jesus had been born. Jerome was clever, but one thing got him into a lot of trouble: he had a really bad temper and didn't always find it easy to get on with people.

One day, Jerome was out walking when he noticed a lion in the distance. As Jerome walked towards the lion, he could see that it was limping. To Jerome's surprise, the lion calmly lay down and held out its paw. Jerome knelt down and saw what was causing the problem. He gently pulled a nasty thorn out of the lion's paw.

Jerome stood up, expecting the lion to stay where it was, but the animal seemed to like the monk who had been so kind to it. The lion also stood up. Jerome took two steps backwards. The lion took two steps backwards. Jerome turned and walked five steps. The lion followed him like a shadow with a big fluffy mane for a head.

The monks who were with Jerome were very nervous of the lion. Jerome became angry with them and insisted that the lion could stay at the monastery. The monks told Jerome that the lion could only stay if it worked for its keep.

Jerome thought about this. The lion could not read or hold a pen, but it could guard the donkey that carried the wood that the monks used for their fires. The donkey had to carry the wood along the road and across the fields. Every day, the lion protected the donkey as it trotted along, but one afternoon, the lion fell asleep and the donkey set off on its own.

That afternoon, some robbers saw the donkey and stole it. When the lion woke up, it was really upset: it was sure that the monks would blame it for the donkey's disappearance. They would think that the lion had eaten the donkey and hidden the bones. This wasn't true, but of course the lion couldn't explain what had really happened. All the monks, including Jerome, were really angry and told the lion that from now on it would have to carry the wood instead.

A few months later, the lion spotted the donkey with some camels. The robbers were returning home from a shopping trip. The lion bounded towards them. When the robbers saw the lion, they fled as fast as they possibly could. They watched from afar as the lion rounded up the camels and the donkey and took them all to the monks. So the lion hadn't eaten the donkey after all! Jerome and the monks realised what had happened and apologised to the lion. At that moment, the robbers arrived with a large amount of oil and offered to buy the camels from the monks. From that day, everyone lived peacefully once again.

Interactive retelling

Dress up a child in a blanket to represent Jerome and mime the story as it unfolds.

Story: Our story is set about 1600 years ago. It is about a man called Jerome. Jerome is a monk who has a very bad temper. He travels around Italy and France with his friends before settling in Bethlehem—the town where Jesus was born. Jerome lives in a monastery with the other monks. He spends much of his day reading the Bible in Hebrew. He is one of the few people who can read Hebrew, so he has an idea—he will write the Bible in a language that many people can understand. That language is called Latin.

Interactive question: Why was it important for the Bible to be written in Latin?

Action: Choose a child to play the part of the lion and mime the story as it unfolds.

Story: Jerome is out for a walk when he comes across a lion. The lion is limping because it has a large thorn in its paw. Jerome gently pulls out the thorn. The lion is full of gratitude. It follows Jerome back to his monastery.

Interactive question: What might the other monks have thought when Jerome turned up at the monastery accompanied by a lion?

Action: Choose three children to be monks.

Story: The monks are very nervous of the lion. Jerome is angry with them and insists that the lion can stay. The monks tell Jerome that the lion can only stay if it works for its keep. The lion cannot read or write, but it can protect the donkey that carries wood for the monks' fire.

Action: Choose a child to play the role of the donkey.

Story: The lion guards the donkey and all is well until, one afternoon, the lion falls asleep.

Action: Choose two children to play the part of the robbers and carefully mime as the story unfolds.

Story: While the lion is asleep, some robbers creep over the hill and steal the donkey. The lion wakes up and panics. It knows the monks will be angry and blame it for eating the donkey—even though this isn't true. As the lion can't talk, it is unable to tell the monks what really happened. All the monks, including Jerome, are really angry and tell the lion that from now on it will have to carry the wood instead.

Interactive questions: What might the outcome have been if Jerome and the other monks had trusted the lion? How might they have behaved when the lion returned alone? How does it feel to be unfairly treated for something we haven't done?

Story: One day, the lion spots the donkey with some camels.

Action: Choose three children to play the role of the camels and act out the story as it unfolds.

Story: The robbers are returning home from a shopping trip. The lion bounds towards them. When the robbers see the lion, they run away as fast as they possibly can. They watch from a distance as the lion rounds up the camels and the donkey and takes them all to the monks. The monks realise that the lion hasn't eaten the donkey after all! Jerome and the monks apologise to the lion. At that moment, the robbers arrive with a large amount of oil and offer to buy the camels from the monks. From that day, everyone lives peacefully once again.

+

— 4 October —

Francis

Teacher's notes

Theme

This assembly is about how people remember us.

Bible link

A child has been born for us. We have been given a son who will be our ruler. His names will be Wonderful Adviser and Mighty God, Eternal Father and Prince of Peace.

ISAIAH 9:6

At Christmas time, many churches hold crib services where people of all ages gather round a Christmas nativity scene to hear the story of Jesus' birth. The crib scene often includes models of animals such as sheep, donkeys, camels and cattle, and characters from the Christmas story—Mary and Joseph, shepherds, wise men and angels. Christians believe that the story of how God would send his Son into the world is foretold by the Old Testament prophet, Isaiah.

Resources

A blanket for Francis to wear, wolf masks or a sign saying 'wolf', a long piece of cloth, figures that might be placed round a nativity crib

Saint in context

Francis of Assisi was born in northern Italy about AD1181. His father sold cloth and was extremely rich. One day, when Francis was recovering from a long illness, he heard a voice telling him to devote the rest of his life to God and to care for people who lived in poverty, as Jesus had done. Francis did as God had asked. Alongside his good works, Francis also loved being on his own and became well known for the way he told the animals in the fields about God. In 1223, just before he died, Francis made the first Christmas nativity scene from wooden figures to help people learn about the Christmas story.

Entry point

Ask the children to think of someone who has recently become famous, such as someone who has won a singing competition on the television. What particular things do the children remember about that person? What would the children like their teachers to remember about them?

Reflection

Talk about different things that we might be remembered for at the end of a single day. What might be the worst thing? How can we make sure that we are remembered for the best thing?

Suggested songs

- Peace, perfect peace (*Come and Praise* 53)
- Make me a channel of your peace (*Come and Praise* 147)
- God made you and me (*Light for Everyone*, SU)

Optional prayer

Dear God, we remember how you came to live on earth, showing us how to love each other. Help us today to be remembered for making good choices in all we do.

'Build a saint' activity

Find a picture of a nativity crib, or make a crib scene using a small empty box. Add the crib to the table as a symbol to remind the children about the story of Francis. Draw pictures of Francis at different stages of his life.

The story retold

Francis of Assisi grew up in northern Italy, 900 years ago. In the town where he lived, a few people were very rich. Others were moderately rich. Some were neither rich nor poor, but most people were living in poverty. Francis' father sold cloth and was very, very rich.

When Francis was growing up, he had everything he needed, but being rich didn't stop Francis becoming ill. He was ill for a long, long time. As he began to get better, he heard a voice telling him to give the rest of his life to God. He was sure it was God speaking directly to him. When he was better, he did not follow his father's trade and sell cloth, but lived with the poorest people in the land and helped them whenever he could.

Other people heard about what Francis was doing and they came to join him. Francis wanted to do what Jesus had done and take care of people in great need. He formed an order of monks who became famous for their work. Francis liked to be on his own, and became famous for talking to animals in the fields surrounding the town where he lived.

One day, Francis visited a place called Gubbio. The people who lived there were afraid of a big wolf that prowled round the city walls. 'Francis,' they said when he arrived, 'go and do something about the wolf. We are so scared of it.'

So, carrying no weapons, Francis and a few others set off towards where the wolf was howling. On seeing the animal's jagged row of teeth, the people with Francis turned and ran away in terror. But Francis carried on walking calmly towards the beast, talking to it as he walked. A while later, he returned to the town with the wolf trotting quietly behind him. 'He's just hungry,' Francis told the townspeople. 'Look after him and he will not harm you.'

Francis longed for people to hear the wonderful stories about all the things Jesus did and said. To help the villagers understand the story of Jesus' birth, Francis built a wooden crib scene with Mary and Joseph and the stable and animals. He used the crib scene to retell the story of Christmas. Francis' idea about having a real crib scene to tell the story of Jesus' birth has lived on. Today, many people have nativity scenes in their houses at Christmas time. Churches, too, have crib scenes so that people can see and remember the story of Christmas.

Interactive retelling

Story: The scene is a town in northern Italy about 900 years ago. It is where Francis of Assisi is growing up. In the town where he lives, a few people are very rich. Others are moderately rich. Some are neither rich nor poor, but most people live in poverty. Francis' father sells cloth and is very, very rich.

Interactive questions: If you had lived 900 years ago, would you have wanted to be one of the very rich people or someone who lived in poverty? Why?

Story: As he grows up, Francis has everything he needs, but being rich doesn't stop Francis becoming ill. He is ill for a long, long time and, as he begins to recover, he hears a voice telling him to give the rest of his life to God. He believes it is God speaking to him. So he decides not to follow his father's trade and sell cloth, but lives with the poorest people in the land and helps them whenever he can.

Interactive questions: What would be the best thing about Francis' new life? What would be the worst thing?

Story: Before long, other people hear about what Francis is doing and come to join him. Francis lives the way Jesus would have lived—simply and with no wealth. Francis and his friends are known as monks. They travel the land, helping people in need.

Interactive question: If Francis and his friends—the Franciscan order of monks—visited our school today, what might they do and who would they help?

Story: One day, Francis and his fellow monks visit a place called Gubbio. The people living there are afraid of a big wolf that prowls round the city walls. 'Francis,' they say when he arrives, 'come and do something about the wolf. We are terrified of it.' So, carrying no weapons, Francis and a few of his friends set off towards where the wolf is howling. On seeing the animal's jagged row of teeth, Francis' friends turn and run away in terror. But Francis carries on alone, walking calmly towards the animal, talking to it as he walks. A while later, he returns to the town with the wolf trotting quietly behind him.

'How have you done that?' everyone asks in amazement. 'He's just hungry,' Francis explains. 'But he's a wolf!' they exclaim. Francis shrugs his shoulders. To him it is obvious. 'Look after him and he will not harm you,' he says.

Interactive question: In what ways can people sometimes be like the wolf?

Story: Francis longs for people to hear the wonderful stories about all the things Jesus did and said. To help the villagers understand the story of Jesus' birth, Francis builds a wooden crib scene with Mary and Joseph and the stable and animals. He uses the crib scene to retell the story of Christmas. Francis' idea about having a real crib scene to tell the story of Jesus' birth has lived on. Today, many people have nativity scenes in their houses at Christmas time. Churches, too, have crib scenes so that people can see and remember the story of Christmas.

Interactive question: Francis used symbols to represent Jesus and his family. What symbols could be used to represent us?

+

— 18 October —

Luke

Teacher's notes

Theme

This assembly is about sharing exciting things.

Bible link

Many people have tried to tell the story of what God has done among us. They wrote what we had been told by the ones who were there in the beginning and saw what happened. So I made a careful study of everything and then decided to write and tell you exactly what took place. Honourable Theophilus, I have done this to let you know the truth about what you have heard.
LUKE 1:1–4

Luke was born in Antioch in Syria. By profession he was a doctor, but he also became a skilled historian, writing both the Gospel named after him and the Acts of the Apostles, which continues the story of what happened to Jesus' followers after the resurrection. He addresses his writings to a person called Theophilus, with the purpose of giving an accurate account of the story of Christianity from Jesus' birth through to the great apostle Paul's arrival in Rome.

Resources

Pictures of incidents from Jesus' life, such as the nativity, his miracles, life in the first century AD, characters from the parables and scenes from his death and resurrection; simple head-dresses (such as three tea towels and means of attaching them); a shawl for Mary

Saint in context

Luke lived at the same time as Jesus, but it is not thought that they ever met. His account of Jesus' life gives precise details about what people said, what they saw and what they heard, so he must have had first-hand access to those who did know Jesus. Sections of Acts are written in the first person, showing that Luke travelled with Paul on some of his missionary journeys. Traditionally, it is thought that Luke lived to the age of 84 and that his tomb is in Ephesus.

Entry point

Encourage the children to think of something exciting that has happened in school recently, and how everyone found out about it. It could be tied in with something the children have achieved.

Reflection

Luke wrote down something he wanted people to know. Think about the most exciting things the children have ever done. Who did they tell? How did they tell them? Did they keep the story to themselves for a while or did they tell everyone straight away? Go on to think about things that the children might want to tell anyone about at the moment.

Suggested songs

- The best gift (*Come and Praise* 59)
- The wise may bring their learning (*Come and Praise* 64)
- He gave me eyes so I could see (*Junior Praise* 74)

Optional prayer

Dear God, thank you that exciting things happen to us that we can share with other people. Thank you that Luke wrote about what happened to Jesus so that we can find out about him.

'Build a saint' activity

Luke was a doctor so he would have had bottles of medicine and potions to give to his patients. Draw a picture of a bottle and on it draw or write about something exciting that the children have shared with others. Add the pictures to the classroom display as a symbol to remind the children about the story of Luke.

The story retold

A doctor from Greece, named Luke, travelled to the same places that Jesus had been to. He asked people questions and wrote down their answers. Perhaps he said, 'Tell me, Mary, you were Jesus' mother. What happened when he was born?' Mary probably thought for a moment and then told Luke about the stable in Bethlehem and how shepherds had arrived with the news that angels had told them Jesus was God's Son. Luke wrote down what Mary said. He thanked her and then went on to see Simon Peter, who had been one of Jesus' closest friends. Peter was a fisherman by trade, but he had travelled with Jesus and seen and heard many of the amazing things Jesus did and said.

Perhaps Simon Peter said, 'We never knew what would happen next. We saw people whose skin was all shrivelled up with leprosy, and they were healed and their skin went back to normal. Then there were people who couldn't walk. When they were brought to Jesus, he had them running and jumping. And add this one to your list—we were out with him on the lake once, and a great storm blew up. We were all terrified, but Jesus stood up in the boat and told the wind and waves to be quiet. And they were. We didn't know what to be more scared of—Jesus or the storm!'

Luke nodded and rolled up the parchment scroll he was writing on. Then he left to see Andrew, who was Peter's brother. 'What sort of things did Jesus say?' Luke asked him. Andrew smiled. 'He told us to love people who didn't like us. That was difficult. And he told us never to judge anyone or think we are better than they are. He told us to put our faith in God before anything else. And he told stories that had a special meaning.'

Luke leaned forward and looked Andrew in the eye. 'What happened at the end?' he asked. 'They killed him,' Andrew said quietly. 'They hung him high up on a wooden cross and they thought they had got rid of him. But he came back to life. It was the most incredible thing imaginable. He spoke to us and ate some food with us. It changed our lives all over again, because, if you've seen someone completely dead and then he's talking and laughing and making barbecues on the beach, you know he is God. Ordinary people just don't do that!'

So Luke completed his account of Jesus' life, as a letter, which he sent to a person called Theophilus. That letter became part of the Bible for people to read because Luke wanted to pass on to others something he had found exciting.

Interactive retelling

Choose three children to play the roles of Luke, Simon Peter and Andrew, and dress them in the head-dresses. Choose someone to play the role of Mary, dressed in a shawl. The children act out the story, using the script as indicated below.

Narrator: A doctor from Greece travels to the same places that Jesus went to. He asks people questions and writes their answers down. Perhaps he says...

Interactive question: What questions would children want to ask about Jesus if they were Luke?

Luke: 'Tell me, Mary, you were Jesus' mother. What happened when he was born?

Narrator: Mary thinks for a moment, then takes a deep breath.

Mary: Jesus was born in a stable in Bethlehem. Then shepherds arrived with the news that angels had told them Jesus was God's Son.

Interactive question: What else do the children know about Jesus' birth?

Narrator: Luke writes down what Mary says. He thanks her and then goes on to see Simon Peter, who had been one of Jesus' closest friends. Peter is a fisherman by trade, but he travelled with Jesus and saw and heard many of the amazing things Jesus did and said.

Simon Peter: We never knew what would happen next. We saw people whose skin was all shrivelled up with leprosy, and they were healed and their skin went back to normal. Then there were people who couldn't walk. When they were brought to Jesus, he had them running and jumping. And add this one to your list—we were out with him on the lake once, and a great storm blew up. We were all terrified, but Jesus stood up in the boat and told the wind and waves to be quiet. And they were. We didn't know what to be more scared of—Jesus or the storm!

Interactive question: What other things do the children know about what Jesus did and said?

Narrator: Luke nods and rolls up the parchment scroll he is writing on. Then he goes on to see Andrew, who is Peter's brother.

Luke: What sort of things did Jesus say?

Narrator: Andrew smiled.

Andrew: He told us to love people who didn't like us. That was difficult. And he told us never to judge anyone or think we are better than they are. He told us to put our faith in God before anything else. And he told stories that had a special meaning.

Interactive question: Do the children know any of Jesus' parables? If not, tell them the parable of the two builders (Luke 6:47–49). The first builder built his house on solid rock and, when the flood came, the house stood up against the rushing water. The second builder didn't build on solid rock and his house was smashed to pieces by the water. The special meaning is that those who listen to Jesus will be on solid ground if they do as he says.

Narrator: Luke leans forward and looks Andrew in the eye.

Luke: What happened at the end?

Andrew: They killed him. They hung him high up on a wooden cross and they thought they had got rid of him. But he came back to life. It was the most incredible thing imaginable. He spoke to us and ate some food with us. It changed our lives all over again, because, if you've seen someone completely dead and then he's talking and laughing and making barbecues on the beach, you know he is God. Ordinary people just don't do that!

Interactive question: Why do Christians believe that Jesus came back to life?

Narrator: So Luke completed his account of Jesus' life, as a letter, which he sent to a person called Theophilus. That letter became part of the Bible for people to read, because Luke wanted to pass on to others something he had found exciting.

+

— 30 November —

Andrew

Teacher's notes

Theme

This assembly is about being scared.

Bible link

'Who is this? He can give orders to the wind and the waves, and they obey him!'
LUKE 8:25B

Andrew spent time with Jesus and saw many of the things that Jesus did. One of those events was when the disciples and Jesus were caught in a storm on Lake Galilee. Jesus stood up in the boat and calmed the storm. The disciples were frightened and amazed.

Resources

A length of brown fabric to create a 'boat' (chairs can be used if brown fabric is not available), blue fabric to create waves, tea towels and old ties to create head-dresses for Jesus and several friends

Saint in context

Andrew is the patron saint of Scotland. He and his brother, Peter, were fishermen by trade, but they were also two of Jesus' closest friends. Although they travelled round with Jesus, they kept their fishing net and boats and still sometimes went out fishing. It is believed that Andrew died for his faith, by crucifixion on an

X-shaped cross. A cross of that shape is now known as St Andrew's cross.

Entry point

Invite the children to share times when they have been really scared and talk about what caused them to be frightened. Can they think of anything that helped them get over their fears?

Reflection

Andrew and the other disciples were very scared, but they had someone to turn to who could help them. Sometimes we have to face things that make us feel afraid. Invite the children to think about someone whom they trust and could ask for help if they were really scared.

Suggested songs

- Call to me (*Light for the World*, SU)
- If I go to the furthest place (*Kidsource* 526)

Optional prayer

Dear God, just as Andrew and the other disciples had you to ask for help, help us to know who we can talk to when there are things that scare us. Help us to remember, also, that you are always with us.

'Build a saint' activity

Make a boat out of modelling clay or playdough to add to the table as a symbol to remind children of the story of Andrew.

The story retold

One evening, Jesus suggested to his friends that they should sail together across Lake Galilee. Lake Galilee lies in a valley, and sometimes winds and rain whistle down the valley, bringing vicious storms that whip up the water.

Jesus and his friends, including Andrew, climbed into one of their fishing boats and set off. It was very peaceful to start with. Everyone was relaxed and laughing together after a busy day. The lake was calm and there were other boats out on the water. After a while, Jesus lay down on a pillow at the back of the boat and went to sleep. His friends chatted to each other as they rowed.

A bank of billowing clouds started to build up in the sky, blocking out the sun. The wind began to blow and the boat felt a little less steady in the water. 'Looks like a storm is on the way,' they said. Andrew and his friends were fishermen. They were used to storms, but this storm was a bad one. It was a 'grit your teeth and hope you survive' sort of storm and the disciples were scared—very scared—especially when the boat began filling with water. The more they baled it out, the more it seemed to slosh over the sides. They were on the verge of sinking.

Where was Jesus while his friends were panicking? There he was—sound asleep with his head resting on a pillow. He must have had a very exhausting day. The frightened friends had to wake him up. 'Master, Master,' they yelled, 'we are about to drown!'

Jesus looked at their wet, frightened faces. Then he calmly stood up and commanded the wind, 'Be quiet!' He said to the waves, 'Be still!' The wind died down and there was a great calm. Jesus said to the disciples, 'Don't you have any faith?'

They were no longer afraid of the storm. That had gone. But they were frightened and amazed about Jesus. They looked at each other and whispered, 'Who is this? He can give orders to the wind and the waves, and they obey him!'

Interactive retelling

Choose children to play the roles of Jesus and several of his friends. Dress the volunteers in tea towel head-dresses. Choose two children to hold the brown fabric to create a boat, behind which the action takes place. (If brown fabric is not available, use chairs.) Choose two children to hold the blue fabric to create waves in front of the boat. The waves need to increase and decrease in strength as dictated by the story.

Story: One evening, Jesus suggests to his friends that they should sail together across Lake Galilee. Lake Galilee lies in a valley, and sometimes winds and rain whistle down the valley, bringing vicious storms that whip up the water.

Interactive question: Why might Jesus have wanted to go across the lake?

Story: Jesus and his friends, including Andrew, climb into one of their fishing boats and set off.

Action: Ask Jesus and his friends to walk behind the brown fabric boat.

Story: It is very peaceful to start with. Everyone is relaxed and they laugh together after a busy day. The lake is calm and there are other boats out on the water. After a while, Jesus lies down on a pillow at the back of the boat and goes to sleep.

Action: Ask the child playing the role of Jesus to put his or her head on one side and pretend to sleep. The children holding the waves create a calm sea.

Story: Jesus' friends chat to each other as they row.

Interactive question: What might the friends have chatted about?

Story: Suddenly, a bank of billowing clouds starts to build up in the sky, blocking out the sun. The wind begins to blow and the boat feels a little less steady in the water. 'Looks like a storm is on the way,' they say.

Interactive question: What might it feel like to be in the middle of a huge lake in a small boat if a storm was brewing?

Story: Andrew and his friends are fishermen. They are used to storms, but this storm is a bad one. It's a 'grit your teeth and hope you survive' sort of storm, and the disciples are scared—very scared—especially when the boat begins to fill with water. The more they bale it out, the more it seems to slosh over the sides. They are on the verge of sinking.

Action: Ask the children playing Jesus' friends to act being scared and baling water out of the boat. Ask the children holding the waves to create a stormy sea.

Story: Where is Jesus while his friends are panicking? There he is—sound asleep with his head resting on a pillow. He must have had a very exhausting day. The frightened friends have to wake him up. 'Master, Master,' they yell, 'we are about to drown!'

Interactive question: What might Jesus do?

Story: Jesus looks at their wet, frightened faces. Then he calmly stands up and commands the wind, 'Be quiet!' He says to the waves, 'Be still!' The wind dies down and there is a great calm.

Action: Ask the cast and the children holding the waves to act out this part of the story.

Story: Then Jesus says to the disciples, 'Don't you have any faith?'

Interactive question: Why might Jesus have asked his friends this question?

Story: They are not frightened of the storm any more. That has gone. Instead, they are frightened about who Jesus might be. They look at each other and whisper, 'Who is this man? Even the wind and the waves obey him.'

Interactive question: For what reasons might Jesus have done this miracle?

+

— 26 December —

Stephen

Teacher's notes

Theme

This assembly is about sacrifices.

Bible link

Jesus said to his disciples, 'If any of you want to be my followers, you must forget about yourself. You must take up your cross and follow me.'

MATTHEW 16:24

Anyone who loves someone will make sacrifices for them. Stephen made the ultimate sacrifice when he was stoned to death for his belief in Jesus' death and resurrection.

Resources

Musical instruments, especially percussion, for children to play to create sound effects for the story

Saint in context

After Jesus returned to heaven, Stephen was chosen by the apostles (Jesus' first disciples) to be one of seven people to take care of widows and give out aid to anyone who needed it. The Bible tells us that Stephen was Jewish by faith but that he could speak Greek. Stephen lived at a time when it was extremely dangerous to join the newfound Christian faith, but he was very bold in telling others about his belief in Jesus. In Greek, Stephen's name means 'crown'.

Entry point

Explore with the children what people do when they support a football team and how they show that their team is really important to them. What do they 'give up' to support their team (for example, Saturday afternoon to watch a match)? Can children think of anything their parents or prime carers give up in order to love and support their children?

Reflection

Stephen gave his whole life for something he believed in. Talk about things that are important enough to make a sacrifice for. Very few of us are asked to give up our lives, but we may be asked to give our time or money.

Suggested songs

- Praise him (*Come and Praise* 40)
- I come like a beggar (*Come and Praise* 90)
- Baking bread (*Songs for Every Assembly*, Out of the Ark Music)

Optional prayer

Dear God, help us to work out what is really important in our lives and whether things are worth making sacrifices for. Be with those who are having a hard time because they are doing what they think is right.

'Build a saint' activity

Draw a picture of the sun with clouds half covering it, to represent the time when Stephen saw the glory of God just before he died. Explore with the children things that the clouds might represent in terms of making sacrifices for something important. For example, in order to learn the five-times table, we might have to make the sacrifice of not watching an episode of a favourite television programme. Write the five-times table on the sun and the television programme on the cloud. Add a picture of a sun with clouds to the classroom display, as a symbol to help children remember the story of Stephen.

The story retold

It was only a short while since Jesus had died on the cross, yet here were people saying he had come back to life again. There was only one thing for it. These people who called themselves Christians must be got rid of. One person in particular, who never stopped talking about Jesus, was a man called Stephen.

A crowd was sent to find Stephen and drag him outside the city, where he was beaten and thrown to the ground. The crowd then made a semicircle around him. There was a strange silence except for the sound of people picking up stones and arranging them into piles. The sun beat down on Stephen's back. There was no escape and he knew it. The crowds were gathering the stones for one reason and one reason alone.

Stephen could feel the anger and hatred coming from the people standing round him. He could see the young man in charge of them, holding their coats. He was the one who cheered the loudest as the first stone was hurled at Stephen.

Stephen lifted his hands over his head to try to protect himself as other stones followed. Soon there was blood trickling down his neck and arms. He wiped it away with the back of his hand. His head was throbbing. Why couldn't the next few minutes be over? Every bone in his body was being pounded and his head felt as if it was about to explode.

Stephen forced his eyes to open. At that moment the sun

broke through the clouds.

'Lord Jesus,' he cried out, 'please welcome me.' Then he pulled himself up on to his knees and gasped as loudly as he could, 'Lord, don't blame them for what they have done!'

Those were Stephen's last words—forgiving those who had killed him. He had given his life for something he believed was the truth. The men who had stoned him went back into the city. The young man who had held the coats was especially pleased with what had happened. His name was Saul, and later he would experience an encounter with God that would completely change his life.

Interactive retelling

Provide a selection of musical instruments and ask children to choose and play a sound effect for the words and phrases shown in bold in the story below. As well as using instruments, children can also create sounds with their mouths. Ask the children to play the sound effect where the ellipses [......] appear in the text. You might want to read the story twice, once as a practice and once as a 'performance'.

Story: It is only a short while since Jesus died on the cross, yet here are people **saying** [......] he has come back to life again. There is only one thing for it. These people who called themselves Christians **must be got rid of**. [......] One person in particular, who never stops talking about Jesus, is a man called Stephen.

Interactive question: Where are the places today where people are not allowed to talk openly about religious beliefs?

Story: A crowd is sent to find Stephen and **drag him outside the city** [......] where he is **beaten and thrown to the ground**. [......] The crowd then make a semicircle around him. There is a strange silence except for the sound of people **picking up stones and putting them into piles**. [......] The sun beats down on Stephen's back. There is no escape and he knows it. The crowds are gathering the stones for one reason and one reason alone. [......]

Interactive question: What might the stones be used for?

Story: Stephen can feel the **anger and hatred** [......] coming from the people standing round him. He can see the young man in charge of them, holding their coats. He is the one who cheers the loudest as **the first stone is hurled** at Stephen. [......]

Stephen lifts his hands over his head to try to protect himself as other stones follow. Soon there is **blood trickling down his neck and arms**. [......] He wipes it away with the back of his hand. **His head is throbbing**. [......] Why can't **the next few minutes** be over? [......] Every bone in his body is being pounded and his head feels as if it is about to explode.

Stephen forces his eyes to open. At that moment **the sun breaks through the clouds**. [......] 'Lord Jesus,' he cries out, 'please welcome me!' Then he pulls himself up on to his knees and gasps as loudly as he can, 'Lord, don't blame them for what they have done!'

Interactive questions: Would it have been easy for Stephen to ask for forgiveness for those who wanted to kill him? Why? Why not?

Story: Those are Stephen's last words—forgiving those who have killed him. He has given his life for something he believes is the truth. The men who have stoned him **go back** into the city. [……] The young man who held the coats is especially pleased with what has happened. His name is Saul, and later he will experience an encounter with God that will completely change his life.

+

— 27 December —

John

Teacher's notes

Theme

This assembly is about talking about other people.

Bible link

Jesus performed many other miracles for his disciples, and not all of them are written in this book. But these are written so that you will put your faith in Jesus as the Messiah and the Son of God. If you have faith in him, you will have true life.
JOHN 20:30–31

It is thought that John, who was one of Jesus' closest friends and the brother of James, probably wrote the fourth Gospel. John used metaphors to describe Jesus, which are like signposts pointing the way to him.

Resources

Pictures of celebrities; a torch; string; objects that have been important in your own life journey, such as photographs, baby items, clothes worn to significant events and so on; a toy sheep; an uncut loaf of bread

Saint in context

John and his brother James were fishermen who worked with their father, Zebedee, up to the moment when Jesus invited them to join him. John had been a follower of John the Baptist and he eagerly followed Jesus. John was very close to Jesus and witnessed many of the things he did, such as bringing Jairus' daughter back to life and the miracle of feeding 5000 people with just five loaves and two small fish. John was beside the cross when Jesus died, and it was John whom Jesus asked to care for Mary, Jesus' mother. John's Gospel is attributed to this close friend of Jesus. John wrote down what he had experienced so that others, too, could put their faith in Jesus.

Entry point

Explore with the children how we might describe well-known celebrities. Is it possible to liken a celebrity to a type of car or an animal? Why? Why not?

Reflection

John painted pictures in people's minds about Jesus. Talk about the kind of pictures someone might paint of us to help others understand what we are like.

Suggested songs

- If I had a hammer (*Come and Praise* 70)
- Break out (*Come and Praise* 91)

Optional prayer

Dear God, thank you for Jesus and for all the things he did. Thank you that John wrote it all down so that we could find out about it all these years later.

'Build a saint' activity

Make a signpost using a straight stick or a piece of dowelling. Cut out a piece of card with an arrow shape at one end and attach it to the top of the stick. Add the signpost to the classroom display as a symbol of John pointing the way to help people understand what Jesus said.

The story retold

Zebedee ran a fishing business, helped by his sons James and John. They were mending their nets one day when Jesus walked by and asked the two brothers to join him as he travelled from place to place, telling people about God. From then on, John and James became close friends of Jesus. They spent their days finding out about him, watching, listening and learning through everything he said and did.

John wrote about many of the important things that happened in Jesus' life. Imagine a line running along in front of you. When you were born is at one end and where you are now is at the other. What important events would be on the line? John wrote in a similar sort of way. John's book was like a signpost, helping people understand the important things about Jesus. John wrote down many of the things he saw Jesus do. Each one tells us something different about Jesus.

John wrote about the time when Jesus went to a wedding where he changed water into wine. John wanted people to know that Jesus was God and could do miracles, as well as showing us that Jesus wanted people to enjoy themselves.

John wrote about how Jesus talked to people whom others turned their backs on—people who had horrible skin diseases and had to live on their own, people who did jobs that made them lonely and in which no one trusted them, and people who were regarded as enemies to be ignored and hated. John wanted us to see that Jesus treated everyone equally and cared about people who were unwell or in any kind of need.

John told stories about Jesus walking across water, calming storms and healing people. These signs show us that Jesus was able to perform miracles and make things happen that wouldn't normally be possible.

John wrote down things that Jesus said about himself using metaphors and pictures—like his picture of being light for the world and a good shepherd who looked after his sheep. Jesus and John both knew that people remember pictures easily.

John wrote down the fact that not everyone liked Jesus or believed what he said. Jesus made enemies of those who were jealous of him or felt threatened by his closeness to God. One day, Jesus was arrested and nailed to a cross. John stood by the cross and watched as Jesus died. Three days later, after Jesus had been laid in a tomb with a heavy stone rolled across the entrance, something extraordinary happened. John went to Jesus' tomb and saw that it was empty. Jesus' body had gone. Later on, John met Jesus after he had risen from the dead. That really was something to write about!

Interactive retelling

Choose several children to form a line.

Story: Imagine there is a line running along the floor. One end of the line represents the time when you were born and the other end represents today. What important events would be on the line?

Action: Ask each child to suggest an important event from a different stage of their life. Ask them to stand in chronological order according to the events suggested. Then ask the children to sit down again.

Story: Zebedee runs a fishing business, helped by his sons James and John. They are mending their nets one day when Jesus walks by and asks the two brothers to join him as he travels from place to place, telling people about God. From then on, John and James become close friends of Jesus. They spend their days finding out about him, watching, listening and learning through everything he says and does.

Action: For each part of the story, invite children to come to the front and mime what Jesus did, then stand in a chronological line.

Story: John writes about many of the important things that happened in Jesus' life—similar to the way we made a line about the important events in our lives—but he doesn't write about Jesus being born in Bethlehem. John's book is like a signpost pointing people towards an understanding of who Jesus is, rather than being an eyewitness account of everything that happened. John writes down many of the things he saw Jesus do, and each one tells us something different about Jesus.

John writes about the time when Jesus went to a wedding, where he changed water into wine. John wants people to know that Jesus is God and can do miracles, as well as showing us that Jesus wants people to enjoy themselves.

Action: The children mime the story of the wedding at Cana, then stand in the chronological line.

Story: John writes about how Jesus talked to people whom others turned their backs on—people who had horrible skin diseases and had to live on their own, people who did unpopular jobs and were isolated and mistrusted, and people who were regarded as enemies to be ignored and hated. John wants us to see that Jesus treated everyone equally and cared about people who were unwell or in any kind of need.

Action: The children mime Jesus talking to everyone.

Story: John tells us stories about Jesus walking across water, calming storms and healing people. These signs show us that Jesus was able to perform miracles and make things happen that wouldn't normally be possible.

Action: The children mime Jesus' actions.

Story: John writes down things Jesus said about himself using metaphors and pictures—like his picture of being a light for the world and a good shepherd who looks after his sheep. Jesus and John both knew that people remember pictures easily.

Action: The children mime what Jesus meant when he said he was the light for the world and the good shepherd.

Story: John writes down the fact that not everyone liked Jesus or believed what he said. Jesus made enemies of those who were jealous of him or felt threatened by his closeness to God.

One day, Jesus is arrested and nailed to a cross. John stands by the cross and watches as Jesus dies. Three days later, after Jesus has been laid in a tomb and a heavy stone rolled across the entrance, something extraordinary happens. John goes to Jesus' tomb and sees that it is empty. Jesus' body has gone. Later on, John meets Jesus after he has risen from the dead. Now that really is something to write about!

Action: The children mime John's role in the story.

Story: John writes down all these things so that we can know about Jesus.

+

— 24 January —

Cadoc

Teacher's notes

Theme

This assembly is about helping others.

Bible link

I will make rivers flow on mountain peaks. I will send streams to fill the valleys. Dry and barren land will flow with springs and become a lake.

ISAIAH 41:18

When Cadoc was a little boy, he learned that God answers prayers in unexpected ways. He came across a really bad situation and, after he had prayed, it changed. Cadoc's experience was similar to the desert imagery used by the prophet Isaiah in Isaiah 41:18: 'Dry and barren land will flow with springs and become a lake.'

Resources

A paper crown, old shawls or blankets, a mouse puppet, white wool, an old sack

Saint in context

Cadoc was born over 1500 years ago, in about AD497. He was the son of a Welsh king called Gwynllwg. When Cadoc grew up, he became a monk and founded a monastery at Llancarfan near Cardiff.

Entry point

There are Christian charities that care for homeless children in many parts of the world. The charities and their supporters pray about the children they will meet before the workers go out on the streets to help them. The story below gives a typical example of the children such charities help.

Edwin's mother spent a lot of time in prison and has now sadly died. His father doesn't want to know him. Edwin was found living on the streets of Guatemala, where he was in a lot of danger from violent people. One day, the charity's street team found him. Over the next few months, they got to know him. He began to trust them and let them help him. Edwin now lives in a home for boys provided by the Christian charity. He has new parents to care for him and is receiving the love that he needs and never thought he would have.

THE TOYBOX CHARITY

There have always been people who need caring for. Talk about projects that the school and individual children have recently supported.

Reflection

Talk about people who might need our help today. What can we do to help? Do we need to ask someone else to help us?

Suggested songs

- Join with us (*Come and Praise* 30)
- When I needed a neighbour (*Come and Praise* 65)
- Would you walk by on the other side? (*Come and Praise* 70)

Optional prayer

Dear God, there are things that we may want to tell you about because they are important to us. Help us to trust that you will answer our prayers in the right way.

'Build a saint' activity

Make a mouse out of modelling clay, or find a toy mouse, and lay a white thread across the classroom display table as a symbol to help children remember the story of Cadoc. Create a picture by drawing a trail of glue on card, then sticking coloured wool on the trail.

The story retold

One day, when Cadoc was a boy, he was out walking and came across a valley near his home where all the houses had been destroyed in a battle. A holy man and some people who had nothing were trying to rebuild one of the houses near an old oak tree. It was very cold and there was not enough food for them.

Cadoc looked at the people struggling to survive. 'Dear God,' he whispered, 'these people need some food. Can you help them?' Cadoc did not know how God would answer his prayer, or even if God had heard him, but he sat down by the oak tree to see if anything would happen.

Suddenly he noticed a little mouse running across the grass in front of him. A few minutes later, the mouse ran back again. Cadoc looked at the little animal. It was clutching something that looked like a grain of wheat between its teeth.

'If there's food,' Cadoc thought, 'that mouse will be back, probably along this path. I will catch him and tie a piece of white thread round his tummy. As the thread unravels, I'll be able to follow him. He might be the answer to my prayer.'

He was! The mouse returned. Cadoc caught him, wrapped a thread round his tummy and let him go. Then Cadoc followed the thread to a tiny hole. He began digging where the hole was and discovered a huge store of grain in the cellar of an old house that had been burnt down during the fighting.

'God answered my prayer,' Cadoc yelled and called to the holy man. 'You've had food here all the time, and the mouse showed me where it was.'

The holy man smiled. He had learnt over the years that when he completely trusted God, somehow things worked out.

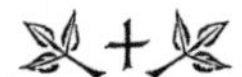

Interactive retelling

Ask the children to sit in two blocks, facing each other, to form a valley in between.

Story: Our story is about a boy called Cadoc, who is the son of a Welsh king. Cadoc is out for a walk.

Action: Choose a child to play the role of Cadoc.

Story: It is a cold winter's day and Cadoc goes to a valley near his home. All the houses have been destroyed in a recent battle. The year is about AD530. Cadoc's clothes are rough against his skin.

Interactive question: What might Cadoc's clothes have been made of?

Story: Cadoc pauses by the burnt-out stump of a tree, and then he walks further into the valley. There he sees a holy man who is helping a group of people to try to rebuild one of the burnt-out houses near an old oak tree.

Action: Choose children to play the roles of a holy man and some villagers.

Story: Cadoc watches them as they break charred wood from the damaged timbers. Maybe they can reuse some of the wood that has survived. It is bitterly cold, but there is no smell of food cooking or any signs of a fire burning. Neither is there any friendly chatter or laugher. The people are struggling.

'Dear God,' Cadoc whispers, 'these people need some food. Can you help them?' Cadoc does not know how God will answer his prayer, or even if God has heard him, but he stays near the oak tree to see if anything will happen.

Interactive question: Cadoc has something in his pocket that will be very useful later to help the people. I wonder what it might be...

Story: Before long, a little mouse scurries across the grass in front of Cadoc.

Action: Choose a child to play the part of the mouse.

Story: A few minutes later, the mouse runs back again. Cadoc looks at the little animal. It is clutching something that looks like a grain of wheat between its teeth.

Interactive question: In what way might the mouse be the answer to Cadoc's prayer?

Story: Suddenly Cadoc knows what to do. His hand reaches into his pocket and his fingers close around a ball of white thread nestled next to the side hem.

'If there's food,' Cadoc thinks, 'that mouse will be back, probably along this path. I will catch him and tie a piece of white thread round his tummy. As the thread unravels, I'll be able to follow him. He might be the answer to my prayer.'

He is! The mouse returns. Cadoc catches him, wraps the thread round his tummy, and lets him go. Cadoc then follows the thread to a tiny hole. He begins digging where the hole is and discovers a huge store of grain in the cellar of an old house that was burnt down during the fighting. 'God answered my prayer,' Cadoc yells. The holy man and the people with him look up, startled by the boy jumping up and down and waving at them.

Interactive question: What might the holy man be thinking?

Story: 'You've had food here all the time, and the mouse showed me where it was,' Cadoc explains. The holy man smiles. Over the years he has learnt that when he completely trusts God, somehow things always work out.

+

— 25 January —

Paul

Teacher's notes

Theme

This assembly is about people in powerful places.

Bible link

'The Spirit is the one who gives life! Human strength can do nothing.'
JOHN 6:63

Saul had an encounter with Jesus that changed his life. His experiences of life as a Christian are recorded in the Acts of the Apostles as well as the many letters he wrote to other Christians and the new churches that emerged. After his encounter, Saul changed his name to Paul and agreed with Jesus' words: 'The Spirit is the one who gives life! Human strength can do nothing.'

Resources

Pictures of the walls of Jerusalem, modern-day Damascus and the surrounding countryside (downloaded from the internet), blankets for Saul and the guards, signs saying 'Damascus' and 'Jerusalem'

Saint in context

Saul lived 2000 years ago. He was born in Tarsus and, as a young man, tried to stamp out Christianity in the early years following Jesus' death and resurrection. One day, Saul was travelling to the city of Damascus when he had a deep experience of God that changed his life. From then on, Saul changed his name to Paul and spent his life telling everyone about Jesus. As a Roman citizen, Paul had many privileges that other believers did not have. He wrote many of the letters that form part of the New Testament.

Entry point

Explore with the children who is the most powerful person they know. Why is that person so powerful? Talk about what makes people powerful and what takes that power away. What power do the children have? Who has power over them? How can power be abused and misused?

Reflection

Talk about things that have made a big difference to our lives, such as a new brother or sister, or moving house. Think of times when we knew something new was going to happen and times when it was unexpected. Talk about good and bad outcomes. Encourage the children to talk to a trusted grown-up about things that may be worrying them.

Suggested songs

- Big, fat, fluffy difference (*Reach Up!* SU)
- Cross over the road (*Come and Praise* 70)
- God in his love (*Come and Praise* 76)
- From the tiny ant (*Come and Praise* 79)

Optional prayer

Dear God, thank you that you are stronger and more powerful than anything in the world and yet you still love each one of us.

'Build a saint' activity

When Saul met God on the way to Damascus, his life was turned upside down and inside out. Find an item of clothing and turn it inside out. Place it on the classroom display table as a symbol to remind the children about the story of Paul.

The story retold

Saul did not like Christians. In fact, he hated them. They caused nothing but trouble with their tiresome talk about Jesus being the Son of God. Just a few years ago, Jesus had been put to death by the Roman authorities, and yet people were saying that he had come back to life again. How ridiculous!

Saul was a powerful person and usually got his own way. He decided to stamp out such talk as quickly as possible, and began to hunt down Jesus' followers and throw them into prison. Saul started in Jerusalem, but he soon heard that there were more of Jesus' followers in the nearby city of Damascus, so he set off to find them.

Saul had almost reached Damascus. He and the men with him were hot and tired. They were looking forward to arriving in the city where they intended to track down the troublemakers. Suddenly, something amazing happened. A bright light flashed around Saul's head. The men with Saul were speechless. All eyes turned towards their leader. Saul had fallen to his knees. His men had heard him fall.

Saul heard a voice saying to him, 'Saul! Saul! Why are you so cruel to me?'

Saul was terrified—so terrified, he could hardly breathe.

'Who are you?' he gasped.

'I am Jesus,' came the reply. 'I am the one you are so cruel to. Now get up and go into the city, where you will be told what to do.'

Saul staggered to his feet, but when he opened his eyes he found that he couldn't see a thing. He had been blinded by the light. One of his men went to his aid, and Saul had to be led by the hand. His plan had been to march into the city in fearsome power, but instead he arrived shaken and unable to see.

For three days, Saul stayed in the city. He neither ate nor drank. After that time, one of the Christians living in the city, a man called Ananias, went to visit him. After Ananias' visit, Saul regained his sight, but he was a changed man. He no longer wanted to hunt down Jesus' followers—he wanted to join them.

Saul became a follower of Jesus and changed his name to Paul. He spent time learning about Jesus and then began to travel wherever he could, telling people what had happened to him and why he now believed that Jesus was the Son of God.

Interactive retelling

Choose a child to play the role of Saul and give him or her a blanket to wear.

Story: After Jesus' death, his followers start to say that Jesus had come back to life again. Saul, who refuses to believe such nonsense, thinks these people are just troublemakers.

Interactive question: Why did Saul hate Jesus' followers so much?

Story: Saul is a powerful person and usually gets his own way. He decides to stamp out such talk as quickly as possible. He begins to hunt down Jesus' followers and throw them into prison. Saul starts in Jerusalem.

Action: Choose a child to hold up the sign 'Jerusalem' on one side of the room and act out Saul putting Jesus' followers in prison.

Story: Soon Saul hears that there are more of Jesus' followers in the nearby city of Damascus, so he sets off to find them.

Action: Choose a child to hold up the sign 'Damascus' on the other side of the room. Choose two children to accompany Saul to Damascus. They set off along the road.

Interactive question: How would Saul and his men have travelled?

Story: Saul has almost reached Damascus. He and the men with him are hot and tired. They are looking forward to arriving in the city where they intend to track down the troublemakers. Suddenly, something amazing happens. A bright light flashes around Saul's head. The men with Saul are speechless. All eyes turn towards their leader. Saul has fallen to his knees. His men heard him fall. Saul hears a voice saying to him…

Action: Choose a child to read the following script.

Jesus: Saul! Saul! Why are you so cruel to me?

Interactive question: How might Saul be feeling at this moment?

Story: Saul is so terrified, he can hardly breathe. 'Who are you?' he gasps.

Jesus: I am Jesus. I am the one you are so cruel to. Now get up and go into the city, where you will be told what to do.

Story: Saul staggers to his feet, but when he opens his eyes he finds that he can't see a thing. He has been blinded by the light. One of his men goes to his aid, and Saul has to be led by the hand. His plan was to march into the city in fearsome power, but instead he arrives shaken and unable to see.

Action: Ask one of the children playing the role of Saul's men to lead Saul by the hand to the city of Damascus.

Interactive question: What difference would an experience like this make to someone's life?

Story: For three days, Saul stays in the city. He neither eats nor drinks. After that time, one of the Christians living in the city, a man called Ananias, goes to visit him. After Ananias' visit, Saul regains his sight, but he is a changed man. He no longer wants to hunt down Jesus' followers—he wants to join them.

Interactive question: What might Ananias' reaction have been when he knew he had to visit Saul?

Story: Saul becomes a follower of Jesus and changes his name to Paul. He spends time learning about Jesus and then begins to travel wherever he can, telling people what has happened to him and why he now believes that Jesus is the Son of God.

+

— 24 February (also 14 May) —

Matthias

Teacher's notes

Theme

This assembly is about stepping into someone else's shoes.

Bible link

They drew names, and Matthias was chosen to join the group of the eleven apostles.

ACTS 1:26

Judas, who was the apostle who betrayed Jesus, bought a field with the money he had earnt by helping to have Jesus arrested. Shortly afterwards, Judas was found dead in the field, having killed himself. Jesus' followers felt that it was right to find someone else to take Judas' place as the twelfth apostle. This person would help the others to spread the news that Jesus had been raised from the dead. Two men were suggested, one of whom was Matthias. Jesus' disciples decided who to choose by the method we might describe as 'drawing lots'. Although this might seem a strange way to make an important decision, it was an accepted form of decision making at that time, and Matthias was thus chosen to join the group of the eleven apostles, making up the twelfth place.

Resources

Simple costume for Matthias, sheets of paper or card, felt-tipped pens, a length of string

Saint in context

Matthias was a contemporary of Jesus. He was probably one of Jesus' friends, although not one of the twelve disciples named by the Gospel writers. Matthias probably witnessed Jesus' death and may have met Jesus after the resurrection. Although very little is known about him, it is apparent that he was considered to be an acceptable replacement for Judas Iscariot, as one of the twelve apostles who were to carry the message about Jesus' life, death and resurrection to different parts of the world.

Entry point

Ask the children whether they have ever stepped into someone else's shoes—for example, as a substitute in a football team, a replacement person to read aloud in assembly, as a replacement to visit someone or go to an event when a friend couldn't go, and so on. How were they chosen? Who did the choosing? What does it mean to 'step into someone else's shoes'?

Reflection

Taking over from someone can be sometimes easy and sometimes difficult. Talk about times when the children have taken over from someone else. Was it easy or difficult? If it was easy, why was this so? What did they have to do? Did they get it right? If it wasn't easy, what made it difficult?

Suggested songs

- Sad, puzzled eyes (*Come and Praise* 74)
- I am planting my feet (*Come and Praise* 103)

Optional prayer

Dear God, taking over when someone else has been doing something can be really difficult. Help us always to do our best when we have the opportunity to step into someone else's shoes.

'Build a saint' activity

Create a timeline with a length of string. On small pieces of card or paper, draw important events in the children's lives when they have stepped into someone else's shoes—for example, playing in the school football team or helping to run the school library. On one piece of card, ask the children to draw the person whose place they took. On another piece of card, ask them to draw themselves in the role they took on. On the reverse side of the first card, ask the children to draw Judas Iscariot. Ask them to draw Matthias on the reverse side of the second card.

Place the cards on the length of string to make a timeline of the events before and after they replaced the original person. Place the timeline on the classroom display table as a symbol to remind the children about the story of how Matthias stepped into Judas Iscariot's shoes.

The story retold

NB: Judas' suicide is deliberately not mentioned in the storytelling.

Matthias was not one of the people that Jesus had chosen to be his twelve closest followers, but it is likely that he had seen everything Jesus did. He might have been on the riverbank the day Jesus was baptised, and in the crowd when Jesus made a blind man see again; he might have overheard Jesus chatting to the people everyone else ignored, and listened to the stories

Jesus told—such as the one about the farmer's son who ran away and then returned home, asking for forgiveness. It must have been an amazing three years in Matthias' life.

Matthias might also have been on that cold, dark hillside when Jesus was nailed to a cross and left to die. That day would have been awful, the worst ever. Jesus had died on a Friday. The next two days must have seemed like a lifetime as Matthias waited with the other disciples, all wondering what they were going to do, now that Jesus was gone. All their hopes and dreams had been shattered. Then, on the Sunday morning, an amazing thing happened: Jesus came back to life. They had seen him die and now here he was again, eating with them, allowing them to touch him, talking to them and reassuring them. Perhaps Matthias had spoken to Jesus and found out for himself that Jesus really had risen from the dead.

Although Matthias wasn't one of Jesus' chosen twelve, he probably wouldn't have minded. He would have been quite happy just being part of the larger crowd of believers. Judas Iscariot was one of the twelve and would have seen everything Jesus did and heard everything Jesus said, just in the way that Matthias had. But Judas allowed himself to listen to Jesus' enemies. He agreed to be paid money in exchange for telling them when Jesus would be away from the crowds. It was Judas' fault that Jesus was arrested and put to death. After Jesus had died, Judas was so upset by what he had done that he left the group and went away by himself.

Now Jesus' friends, who became the apostles, had to find someone to replace Judas. Peter took charge. First they prayed and asked God to help them. Then they wrote down the names of the two people who they thought could take over from Judas, and Matthias was one of them. When Matthias' name was chosen, his life changed completely. Working with the other eleven apostles, he began to tell people about Jesus. He also made sure people in need were helped, money was given out fairly and that what Jesus had said and done was passed on to others. It was a huge responsibility, but Matthias was ready for it and everyone helped to make it as easy as possible for him. For Matthias, stepping into Judas' shoes seemed a natural thing to do.

Interactive retelling

Choose a child to play the role of Matthias. Give the child a 'robe' to wear and ask him or her to sit in a chair at the front of the group (the hot seat). The child playing Matthias can ask other children to help with the answers. As the questions are answered, invite a volunteer to draw a quick sketch of that part of the story, using a thick felt-tipped pen. As the pictures are built up, create a timeline of the events.

Whole group question:	Matthias, what did you see Jesus do?
Hot seat answers:	I saw him performing miracles (such as healing a blind man), telling stories (such as the story of the farmer's son), and chatting to the people everyone else ignored.

Whole group question:	What was the very worst day for you and Jesus' other friends?
Hot seat answers:	Seeing Jesus being arrested, tried and hung on a cross to die.
Whole group question:	What was the very best day for you?
Hot seat answers:	Seeing Jesus after he came back to life, eating with him, talking to him, touching him and hearing him reassure us.
Whole group question:	What did Judas do?
Hot seat answers:	Judas was one of Jesus' twelve chosen people. He'd been with Jesus, just as I had, but Judas listened to Jesus' enemies. He agreed to be paid money in exchange for telling them when Jesus would be away from the crowds. After Jesus had died, Judas was so upset by what he had done that he went away by himself.
Whole group question:	So what happened next?
Hot seat answers:	Jesus' friends, who were now known as the apostles, had to find someone to replace Judas. Peter took charge.

Whole group question: How did Peter and the others decide who would replace Judas?

Hot seat answers: First they prayed and asked God to help them. Then they wrote down the names of the two people who they thought could take over from Judas, and my name was one of them.

Whole group question: What happened next?

Hot seat answers: My name was chosen.

Whole group question: How did you feel, stepping into Judas' shoes?

Hot seat answers: My life changed completely. Working with the other eleven apostles, I began to tell people about Jesus. I also made sure people in need were helped, money was given out fairly and that what Jesus had said and done was passed on to others. It was a huge responsibility, but I was ready for it and everyone helped to make it as easy as possible for me. For me, stepping into Judas' shoes seemed a natural thing to do.

+

— 1 March —

David

Teacher's notes

Theme

This assembly is about the stories people tell about us.

Bible link

'Good people bring good things out of their hearts.'
MATTHEW 12:35A

David is the patron saint of Wales. In stories about him, he always reflects the verse in Matthew's Gospel where Jesus explains that people's words show what is in their hearts.

Resources

Pictures of bees, a picture of a monastery, a map of South Wales, some honey

Saint in context

David lived around AD520 to 589. He founded twelve monasteries in South Wales. David became the patron saint of Wales and was known for his teaching and good works. His monastic rule included a diet of only bread and water, pulling the plough without animals to help and spending every evening in prayer, reading or writing. David died on 1 March, which is now St David's day.

Entry point

Ask the children to give three facts about someone who is well known to them, such as a celebrity, someone in school or someone in the local community. Ask the whole group to see if they can guess who is being described.

Reflection

People remembered the story about David and Domnoc and the bees and told others about it. People have memories of things we have done, too, and will tell others stories about us. Invite the children to think of a happy memory or story that is special to them.

Suggested songs

- Bread for the world (*Come and Praise* 75)
- It's a new day (*Come and Praise* 106)

Optional prayer

Dear God, thank you for all the stories I have heard about people doing kind and generous things to help others. May stories like that be the ones told about me, too.

'Build a saint' activity

Give out sheets of yellow paper and sheets of black paper. Ask the children to draw or write stories about kind things they have done recently. Use silver pens or white chalks on the black paper. Arrange the sheets in alternating colour order to represent a bee's stripes. Add thin strips of black paper to represent the bee's legs and antennae. Add a picture of a bee to the display and place it on the classroom display table as a symbol to remind the children of the story of David.

The story retold

David was born in Wales around AD520: no one is sure of the exact date. He spent much of his life praying and going without food in order to concentrate on God. When he did eat, his diet was mostly leeks and bread, and he drank only water. David founded twelve monasteries in South Wales. He spent time in each monastic community, teaching the monks how to pray and live godly lives. The monasteries were built near the sea so that visitors could visit, but they also had to be hidden away so that pirates sailing by could not see them. David was such a shining example of how to live a good life that he became the patron saint of Wales.

There is a story that grew up about David and a swarm of bees. One of the monks who worked with him was an Irishman called Domnoc. For many years, Domnoc's job was to look after the bees, until the day came when he had to return to Ireland. He said goodbye to the monks and then to the bees he had cared for, and headed for his boat.

But the bees were not going to let him go so easily. Suddenly there was a huge buzzing noise in the air. Here was trouble! The bees had decided to go with him. Leaving the boat on the shore, Domnoc took the bees back to their hives, but no sooner had he returned to his boat than the air was filled once more with the yellow and black honey-makers. What was Domnoc to do?

David was visiting the monastery at the time and heard about what was happening. He knew just what to do and gave the bees as a present to Domnoc. Domnoc and his bees left in peace—well, as much peace as sailing with a swarm of bees would allow. It is said that all bees in Ireland are, even today, descended from Domnoc's bees.

Interactive retelling

Ask the children to act out the story as indicated below.

Story: David is born around…

Action: Hold fingers up to represent 520.

Story: He grows up in Wales and spends much of his life praying and going without food in order to concentrate on God.

Action: Put hands together and keep mouth closed.

Story: He eats leeks and bread and drinks only water.

Action: Mime eating leeks and bread and drinking only water.

Story: David founds twelve monasteries in South Wales. He spends time in each monastic community, teaching the monks how to pray and live godly lives. The monasteries are built near the sea so that visitors can visit, but they also have to be hidden away so that pirates sailing by cannot see them.

Action: Make wave actions with hands.

Story: David becomes the patron saint of Wales.

Action: Mime being David as the patron saint, going around doing good. Ask children for suggestions about what he did.

Story: There is a story about David and a swarm of bees. One of the monks who works with David is an Irishman called Domnoc. For many years, Domnoc's job is to look after the bees.

Action: Mime Domnoc looking after the bees.

Story: The day finally arrives when Domnoc has to return to Ireland. He says goodbye to the monks and then to the bees he has cared for, and heads for his boat.

Action: Mine Domnoc saying goodbye to the monks and the bees and heading for his boat.

Story: But the bees are not going to let him go so easily. Suddenly there is a huge buzzing noise in the air. Here is trouble! The bees have decided to go with him. Leaving the boat on the shore, Domnoc takes the bees back to their hives.

Action: Mime the bees following Domnoc to his boat, and then Domnoc taking them back to their hives.

Story: But no sooner has Domnoc returned to his boat than the air is filled once more with the yellow and black honey-makers. What is Domnoc to do?

Action: Mime Domnoc being followed back to his boat by the bees and then scratching his head, wondering what to do.

Story: David is visiting the monastery at the time and he hears about what is happening. He knows what to do and gives the bees as a present to Domnoc. They all leave in peace—well, as much peace as sailing with a swarm of bees will allow.

Action: Attempt a 'Mexican bee buzz', buzzing quietly on one side of the room and spreading the buzz across to the other side of the room.

Story: It is said that all bees in Ireland are, even today, descended from Domnoc's bees.

+

— 17 March —

Patrick

Teacher's notes

Theme

This assembly is about who we trust.

Bible link

The Lord has given you trouble and sorrow as your food and drink. But now you will again see the Lord, your teacher, and he will guide you.
ISAIAH 30:20

Patrick's life was one of hardship. He was a slave and later lived in poverty as a monk, yet still he had a tremendous faith in God. Patrick would have understood the teaching in the book of the Old Testament prophet, Isaiah, which tells us that God will make us go through hard times, but he himself will be there to teach us.

Resources

A toy snake, a picture of a shamrock, an outline map of the UK, a blanket for Patrick

Saint in context

Patrick is the patron saint of Ireland, even though he was born not in Ireland but in Wales, in about AD387. When he was a teenager, he was captured by pirates and taken to Ireland, where he was sold as a slave. Life was tough but after approximately six years he escaped and returned to Wales, where he entered the Church. Later, he returned to Ireland, where he worked in churches, caring for those who were unwell and teaching people about God. It is believed that he died on 17 March.

Entry point

Explore what it means to trust someone and why it is important to have people we can trust in our lives. Ask the children to think of different situations when they have to trust teachers, friends, team members and family members. What makes someone trust somebody else?

Reflection

Talk about people the children trust and why they trust those people. Can other people trust us? Why? Why not?

Suggested songs

- The Lord is my shepherd (*Come and Praise* 56)
- Spirit of peace (*Come and Praise* 85)
- If I go to the furthest place (*Songs for Every Assembly*, Out of the Ark Music)

Optional prayer

Dear God, sometimes things happen that make us unhappy. Show us who we can trust so that we can tell them about whatever is making us unhappy.

'Build a saint' activity

Make a snake out of modelling clay and add it to the classroom display table as a symbol to remind the children about the story of Patrick. Alternatively, ask the children to think about how a snake sheds its skin and then draw an outline of the snake leaving its skin.

On the snake, ask the children to draw or write about something unpleasant that happened, and what happened next because someone they trusted helped them.

The story retold

Patrick was born over 1600 years ago, probably in Wales, but definitely not in Ireland. When Patrick was a teenager, a pirate ship moored up near where he lived. The pirates grabbed hold of him and dragged him to their ship. Patrick was alone and very scared. He was taken to Ireland to be sold as a slave—which meant that he had to work very hard, do what he was told, have little to eat, never complain and expect to be beaten. Life was hard and not much fun.

Patrick remained a slave for a long, long time. The only thing that helped him through those times was his faith in God. He longed to get away but never managed to escape. Then, some years later, when he was 23 years old, his chance came. Think what it must have felt like to run free and leave captivity behind. Patrick made his way to the coast and found a boat that took him back home. The next thing we know about him is that he became a priest, working in a church.

Later, Patrick chose to go back to Ireland. He wanted people to understand what God was like, so he took an Irish shamrock, which is a plant that has its leaves divided into three parts. 'This leaf is like the Christian God,' he would say. 'Three in one and one in three. God the Father, God the Son and God the Holy Spirit.' People remembered what he said.

Stories grew up about Patrick's life in Ireland. A story is told about snakes that were eating cattle and sheep. Patrick was called in to get rid of them. As he approached them, the snakes slithered off into a nearby lake. Patrick stood by the side of the lake and, with a great sense of trust, prayed to God. Before long, the waters of the lake began to burn. Small flames quickly became a roaring blaze. The snakes were about to be barbecued! They had no option, if they were to survive, but to sneak out of the lake. Patrick watched as they did just that. He smiled as they moved away from him and headed for the open sea, never to be heard of again.

Perhaps because of the horrible time he had when he was growing up, Patrick was always humble and trusted God for absolutely everything.

Interactive retelling

Ask the children to act out the story using their fingers as directed in the text.

Story: Patrick was born over 1600 years ago, probably in Wales, but definitely not in Ireland. Patrick is in his teens when a pirate ship moors up near where he lives.

Action: Ask for suggestions about what Patrick might have been doing when the pirate ship arrived and finger-mime the answers. (For example, fetching water, playing football, eating.)

Story: The pirates grab hold of Patrick and drag him to their ship.

Action: Cup hands to make a boat.

Story: Patrick is alone and very scared. He is taken to Ireland to be sold as a slave—which means that he has to work very hard, do what he is told, have little to eat, never complain and expect to be beaten. Life is hard and not much fun.

Action: 'Thumbs down' sign. Ask the children to suggest how Patrick might be feeling and why. (For example, he is lonely because he has no friends.)

Story: Patrick remains a slave for a long, long time. The only thing that helps him through those times is his faith in God.

Action: Traditional sign of praying (hands together).

Story: Patrick longs to get away but never manages to escape. Then some years later, when he is 23 years old, his chance comes. Think what it must feel like to run free and leave captivity behind.

Action: Run fingers along arm and jump fingers up and down.

Story: Patrick makes his way to the coast and finds a boat that takes him back home. The next thing we know about him is that he becomes a priest, working in a church.

Action: Invite a child to come to the front and play the role of Patrick. Use the hot-seating technique to find out how Patrick felt, how he escaped, what it felt like to be free, why he decided to become a priest and what he thinks he will do next.

Story: Later, Patrick chooses to go back to Ireland. He wants people to understand what God is like, so he takes an Irish shamrock, which is a plant that has its leaves divided into three parts. 'This leaf is like the Christian God,' he says. 'Three in one and one in three. God the Father, God the Son and God the Holy Spirit.' People remember what he says.

Action: Ask three children to come to the front, stand with their backs together and make the shape of a shamrock's leaves with their arms.

Story: Stories grow up about Patrick's life in Ireland. A story is told about snakes that are eating cattle and sheep.

Action: Act out snakes on one hand grabbing the cattle on the other.

Story: Patrick is called in to get rid of them. As he approaches them, the snakes slither off into a nearby lake. Patrick stands by the side of the lake and, with a great sense of trust, prays to God. Before long, the waters of the lake begin to burn. Small flames quickly become a roaring blaze. The snakes are about to be barbecued! They have no option, if they are to survive, but to sneak out of the lake. Patrick watches as they do just that. He smiles as they move away from him and head for the open sea, never to be heard of again.

Action: Rest fingers and hands.

Story: Perhaps because of the horrible time he had while he was growing up, Patrick remains always humble and trusts God for absolutely everything.

+

— 19 March —

Joseph

Teacher's notes

Theme

This assembly is about making decisions.

Bible link

A young woman named Mary was engaged to Joseph from King David's family. But before they were married, she learnt that she was going to have a baby by God's Holy Spirit.
MATTHEW 1:18B

Joseph was someone who trusted God and took all the things that happened to him as part of God's plan for his life. In the Bible, his entry to the Christmas story is simple: he was the man engaged to be married to Mary, the young woman whom God had chosen to give birth to his Son, Jesus.

Resources

Simple costume for Joseph, hammer, handsaw, nails and other non-electric tools that Joseph might have used as a carpenter, a ring of tinsel to go round the angel's head

Saint in context

The Gospel writers Matthew and Mark both refer to Jesus as 'the son of the carpenter' (Matthew 13:55; Mark 6:3). As a carpenter, Joseph was important to the community in Nazareth where he lived because he provided tools and furniture. He would have passed his skills on to Jesus. The Gospel writers also record that Joseph and Mary had other children, mentioning that Jesus had brothers and sisters.

Entry point

Ask the children what important decisions they have had to make. In pairs or together as a group, ask them to share what options were open to them, what they chose to do and the outcome of their choice.

Reflection

Talk about difficult decisions we have to make. Think about times when the children have talked to others before making a decision, and times when they have made a decision on their own. What happened afterwards?

Suggested songs

- One more step along the world I go (*Come and Praise* 47)
- To everything, turn, turn, turn (*Come and Praise* 113)
- There's a time to laugh (*Songs for Every Assembly*, Out of the Ark Music)

Optional prayer

Dear God, sometimes we have to make decisions and don't know what is the best choice. Remind us that you can guide us if we trust you and ask you what to do.

'Build a saint' activity

Ask the children to cut out a large question mark from paper. On one side, write a sentence about a decision they have had to make. On the other side, write what happened as a result of the decision.

Draw a saw (that Joseph would have used) at the bottom of the question mark and add it to the classroom display table as a symbol to remind the children of the story of Joseph.

The story retold

Joseph was a carpenter. He lived in Nazareth and was looking forward to marrying a young girl called Mary, to whom he was engaged. Meanwhile, he was working hard in his carpenter's workshop. He was proud of the beautiful pieces of farm equipment and furniture he made.

Joseph was also proud of the family he came from. His great-great-great- (and a lot more greats) grandfather had been King David himself. That made Joseph's family very special.

One day, Joseph's life was turned upside down. An angel had visited Mary and told her she was going to have a baby. Now that really was a surprise! Joseph tossed and turned in his bed. How was he going to deal with Mary's news without the whole town disapproving of her? Perhaps he shouldn't marry her after all... or perhaps he should. It was such an important decision to have to make. Joseph prayed about it; he thought about it; he was having difficulty going to sleep because of it.

Eventually, Joseph fell asleep. It was then that God had a little word with him: an angel spoke to Joseph in a dream. The angel said, 'Joseph, the baby that Mary will have is from the Holy Spirit. Go ahead and marry her. Then after the baby is born, name him Jesus, because he will save people from their sins.'

Joseph sat up in bed. God had spoken to him. Of that he

had no doubt, and now he knew what to do. The decision was easy. He left his bed and walked round to Mary's house to tell her what he had decided to do. Joseph trusted God and he trusted Mary. He would marry her and take great care of both her and the tiny baby who was the Son of God.

Interactive retelling

Choose a child to play the role of Joseph and give him or her the dressing-gown or coat to wear. Ask the child to role-play working in a carpenter's workshop and explore the sort of things Joseph would have made.

Story: Joseph is a carpenter. He lives in Nazareth and is looking forward to marrying a young girl called Mary, to whom he is engaged. Meanwhile, he is working hard in his carpenter's workshop. He is proud of the beautiful pieces of farm equipment and furniture he makes.

Joseph is also proud of the family he comes from. His great-great-great- (and a lot more greats) grandfather is King David himself. That makes Joseph's family very special.

Action: Ask the children if they can name the first few people in their family tree (their parents and grandparents).

Story: One day, Joseph's life is turned upside down. An angel visits Mary and tells her she is going to have a baby. Now that really is a surprise!

Action: Role-play the angel Gabriel's visit to Mary. The story can be found in Luke 1:26–38.

Story: Joseph tosses and turns in his bed. How is he going to deal with Mary's news without the whole town disapproving of her? Perhaps he shouldn't marry her after all… or perhaps he should. It is such an important decision to have to make. Joseph prays about it; he thinks about it; he is having difficulty going to sleep because of it.

Action: Ask the children what keeps them awake at night.

Story: Eventually, Joseph falls asleep. It is then that God has a little word with him: an angel speaks to Joseph in a dream.

Action: Ask the child playing Joseph to lie down and act out the angel's visit. Choose a child to play the role of the angel and say the following lines.

Angel: Joseph, the baby that Mary will have is from the Holy Spirit. Go ahead and marry her. Then after the baby is born, name him Jesus, because he will save people from their sins.

Story: Joseph sits up in bed. God has spoken to him. Of that he has no doubt, and now he knows what to do. The decision is easy. He leaves his bed and walks round to Mary's house to tell her what he has decided to do.

Action: Create freeze-frames for each of the following short sentences. Pay particular attention to the facial expressions of the children taking part.

Story: Joseph trusts God.

Joseph marries Mary.

Joseph learns that he has to go to Bethlehem to register his name in the Roman census.

Joseph travels to Bethlehem with Mary.

The town is full. There is no room for them in the inn.

Mary's baby is born in a stable.

Joseph takes care of the tiny baby who is the Son of God.

+

— 20 March —

Cuthbert

Teacher's notes

This assembly is about life-changing events.

Bible link

'Look at the crows! They don't plant or harvest, and they don't have storehouses or barns. But God takes care of them. You are much more important than any birds.'
LUKE 12:24

Like all of us, Cuthbert experienced events that changed his life. Through all the changes, he trusted that God would look after him. He became a monk and bishop in the Church and learned the meaning of Jesus' words not to worry about our lives because God will take care of us.

Resources

Map of north-east England and Scotland, showing the places Cuthbert travelled to during his life (Melrose, Lindisfarne, Farne Islands); the names of the three places written out for children to hold up; pictures of a salmon, an eagle, some seals and some seagulls; a simple costume for Cuthbert

Saint in context

Cuthbert was an Anglo-Saxon. He was born in about AD636 and lived in the north-east of England. He was a shepherd boy during his teenage years, then a soldier and a monk, before becoming a bishop in Northumbria (which, in those days, included south-east Scotland and most of north-east England). Cuthbert enjoyed solitude and lived for many years on the Island of Lindisfarne and the nearby Farne Islands. His life was recorded by a scholar and monk by the name of Bede.

Entry point

Ask the children what we mean by a 'life-changing experience'. Ask them to think whether they have ever had such an experience—such as a baby brother or sister being born into their family. Ask them to share their memories of the experience if they are happy to do so.

Reflection

Cuthbert faced many changes in his life. Talk about important changes the children have faced. Talk about other changes they will face as they grow up. What helps us when everything around us is changing?

Suggested songs

- The journey of life (*Come and Praise* 45)
- Monday morning (*Songs for Every Assembly*, Out of the Ark Music)

Optional prayer

Dear God, when changes happen in our lives, help us to cope with what is happening, and give us a greater faith in you.

'Build a saint' activity

The eagle dropping a fish near Cuthbert when he was so tired and hungry helped his faith to grow so that he trusted God even more to look after him. Add a picture of an eagle to the classroom display table as a symbol to remind the children of the story. Cut out fish, and on each one draw or write about a change that the children are facing or will have to face in the near future.

The story retold

Cuthbert was born in AD636. That's more than 1400 years ago. He grew up to be a shepherd and lived in the north-east of England. One night, he had a vision in which he saw bright lights flashing across the sky. On the same night, the holy bishop, Aidan, died in nearby Bamburgh. The two events coming together had a huge effect on Cuthbert and he couldn't find peace until he decided to give his life to God and become a monk. He travelled to Melrose in Scotland to join the abbey there.

Some years later, Cuthbert was out for a walk when he got lost. He was very tired and hungry and there was no one around to help him—but he still had his faith in God. Cuthbert prayed to God for help. Suddenly, an eagle glided into view, carrying a huge salmon in its talons. The fish was too heavy for the eagle and the bird dropped it close to where Cuthbert was standing. With great excitement, and his faith in God strengthened, Cuthbert ate some of the salmon and then set the rest of the fish down on the ground so that the eagle could share the meal.

For many years, Cuthbert travelled, all the time meeting new people, going to new places and telling people about his faith. His life constantly changed until he returned to Melrose in Scotland to be in charge of the monks there. He made wise decisions and the monastery at Melrose grew.

Cuthbert wanted to be on his own, though, so that he

could spend more time praying. He changed his life once more and headed south to Lindisfarne, which is also called Holy Island. Although only a few people lived there, they were still too many for Cuthbert, so he moved to the Farne Islands, where his only companions were the birds and seals. Even then, people kept visiting him to ask his advice and questions about their faith, so Cuthbert built a landing-stage for visitors to moor their boats and a small house for them to stay in.

Later, he returned to Lindisfarne, where he became a bishop. He died on his beloved Farne Islands when he was very old and frail. The island is now a protected place for birds and seals.

Interactive retelling

Choose a child to play the part of Cuthbert and give him or her the coat to wear. Also choose some volunteers to hold the place names and pictures as indicated in the resources list above. When each place name or item is mentioned, the child holding that place name or picture hands it to Cuthbert. Show the children a map and point out the places that Cuthbert travelled to during his life.

Story: Cuthbert was born in AD636. That's more than 1400 years ago. He grows up to be a shepherd and lives in the north-east of England. One night, he has a vision in which he sees bright lights flashing across the sky. On the same night, the holy bishop, Aidan, dies in nearby Bamburgh. The two events coming together have a huge effect on Cuthbert and he can't find peace until he decides to give his life to God and become a monk. He travels to Melrose in Scotland to join the abbey there.

Interactive question: What daily activities do monks carry out?

Story: Some years later, Cuthbert is out for a walk when he gets lost. He is very tired and hungry and there is no one around to help him—but he still has his faith in God. Cuthbert prays to God for help. Suddenly, an eagle glides into view, carrying a huge salmon in its talons. The fish is too heavy for the eagle, and the bird drops it close to where Cuthbert is standing. With great excitement, and his faith in God strengthened, Cuthbert eats some of the salmon and then sets the rest of the fish down on the ground so that the eagle can share the meal.

Interactive question: What three words best describe how Cuthbert's feelings might have changed over the short period of time when he was lost?

Story: For many years, Cuthbert travels, all the time meeting new people, going to new places and telling people about his faith. His life constantly changes until he returns to Melrose in Scotland to be in charge of the monks there. He makes wise decisions and the monastery at Melrose grows.

Interactive questions: Do you think Cuthbert preferred to travel or to be in one place all the time? Why?

Story: Cuthbert wants to be on his own, though, so that he can spend more time praying. He changes his life once more and heads south to Lindisfarne, which is also called Holy Island. Although only a few people live there, they are still too many for Cuthbert.

Interactive question: What decisions can people make to help them live together and get on with each other?

Story: Cuthbert moves to the Farne Islands, where his only companions are the birds and seals. Even then, people keep visiting him to ask his advice and questions about their faith, so Cuthbert builds a landing-stage for visitors to moor their boats and a small house for them to stay in.

Interactive question: What questions would you ask Cuthbert?

Story: Later, Cuthbert returns to Lindisfarne, where he becomes a bishop. He dies on his beloved Farne Islands when he is very old and frail. The island is now a protected place for birds and seals.

+

— 25 March —

Mary

Teacher's notes

Theme

This assembly is about Christmas.

Bible link

Mary said: 'With all my heart I praise the Lord, and I am glad because of God my Saviour. He cares for me, his humble servant. From now on, all people will say God has blessed me.'
LUKE 1:46–48

After Mary learnt from the angel Gabriel that she was to be the mother of God's Son, she went to visit her cousin Elizabeth, who was also expecting a baby. Mary was so excited by her news that she sang a song of praise to God. This song is now very famous and is known as the Magnificat. It is frequently said or sung in Christian church services.

Resources

Various pictures of Mary, both fine and modern art, downloaded from the internet

Saint in context

Mary was an ordinary Jewish girl who lived in Nazareth in Galilee. Her family was descended from King David. One day, the angel Gabriel visited Mary, bringing the news that she would have a baby.

Mary was engaged to be married to Joseph, who was the village carpenter, but her baby would be God's Son. Mary gave birth to Jesus in Bethlehem. Thirty-three years later, she would watch him die on a cross outside the city walls of Jerusalem.

Entry point

Show the children pictures of Mary and discuss together what she might be doing or thinking. What is the artist trying to say about her? Ask the children to think of two people they trust and then to share why they trust those people.

Reflection

Talk about times when we have to trust someone. Does trusting someone change the way we think about him or her? Are friendships stronger or weaker because of the trust?

Suggested songs

- I want to see your baby boy (*Come and Praise* 117)
- The virgin Mary (*Come and Praise* 121)
- Mary had a baby (*Come and Praise* 123)

Optional prayer

Dear God, thank you that Mary trusted you. Help us to do the same, even when we don't understand what is happening in the world around us.

'Build a saint' activity

Make an angel by first cutting out a circle from paper or thin card. Cut a straight line into the centre (along the radius) and then create a cone shape by sliding one edge of the radius under the other and securing with sticky tape. Fold a piece of paper in half and cut out a pair of symmetrical wings. On the wings, write the angel

Gabriel's words to Mary: 'You will have a son and his name will be Jesus.' Place the angels on the classroom display table as a symbol to remind the children about the story of Mary.

The story retold

Mary was very young—probably still in her teens—when God chose her to be the mother of his only Son. She was an ordinary girl from an ordinary family, looking forward to an ordinary marriage to an ordinary man named Joseph, who was an ordinary carpenter in the ordinary town of Nazareth.

Mary would never forget the moment when her life was turned upside down. It began when the angel Gabriel dropped in. She knew that angels sometimes visited people—they were messengers from God—but she never expected one to come to see her.

'Don't be afraid!' the angel said as Mary's mouth opened very wide and the biggest gasp she had ever gasped fell from her lips. 'God is pleased with you and you will have a son. His name will be Jesus. He will be great and will be called the Son of God Most High.'

This was no longer an ordinary day and Mary was no longer an ordinary person. For one thing, she had to have an extraordinary amount of faith in order to trust God enough to let him take care of her and her baby, and to sort everything out for her (which he did).

Joseph stood by Mary when she told him what had happened. He too had an extraordinary faith and trust in God, especially when they discovered that they were going to have to travel all the way to Bethlehem shortly before Mary's baby was due to be born. Joseph and Mary were both descended from King David, and, when the Romans wanted to raise money for their army, they ordered everyone to go to the town of their ancestors to register and be taxed. So to Bethlehem Joseph and Mary had to go. While they were there, Mary's baby was born. They named him Jesus, just as the angel had said.

Soon after Jesus was born, Mary and Joseph had some visitors. Shepherds, who had also been visited by angels, came to the stable to see the baby. Later on, wise men who had travelled for miles to bring gifts of gold, frankincense and myrrh also visited the little family. Mary trusted God. He had looked after her and would help her to care for her very special baby.

Interactive retelling

Ask the children to listen to the story—retold in the present tense—and then to answer the questions on page 116. This could be a quiz.

Story: Mary is very young—probably still in her teens—when God chooses her to be the mother of his only Son. She is an ordinary girl from an ordinary family, looking forward to an ordinary marriage to an ordinary man named Joseph, who is an ordinary carpenter in the ordinary town of Nazareth.

Mary will never forget the moment when her life turns upside down. It begins when the angel Gabriel drops in. She knows that angels sometimes visit people—they are messengers from God—but she never expected one to come to see her.

'Don't be afraid!' the angel says as Mary's mouth opens very wide and the biggest gasp she has ever gasped falls from her lips. 'God is pleased with you and you will have a son. His name will be Jesus. He will be great and will be called the Son of God Most High.'

This is no longer an ordinary day and Mary is no longer an ordinary person. For one thing, she has to have an extraordinary amount of faith in order to trust God enough to let him take care of her and her baby, and to sort everything out for her (which he does).

Joseph stands by Mary when she tells him what has happened. He too has an extraordinary faith and trust in God, especially when they discover that they are going to have to travel all the way to Bethlehem shortly before Mary's baby is due to be born. Joseph and Mary are both descended from King David, and, when the Romans want to raise money for their army, they order everyone to go to the town of their ancestors to register and be taxed. So to Bethlehem Joseph and Mary have to go. While they are there, Mary's baby is born. They name him Jesus, just as the angel has said.

Soon after Jesus is born, Mary and Joseph have some visitors. Shepherds, who have also been visited by angels, come to the stable to see the baby. Later on, wise men who have travelled for miles to bring gifts of gold, frankincense and myrrh also visit the little family. Mary trusts God. He has looked after her and will help her to care for her very special baby.

Questions

1. Who is Mary engaged to?
2. Where do they live?
3. What is the name of the angel who comes to visit Mary?
4. What are angels?
5. What is Mary's son to be called?
6. Where do Mary and Joseph have to travel to?
7. Why do they have to travel there?
8. Who are the first people to visit Jesus?
9. What three gifts do the wise men bring with them?
10. What age was Jesus when he died?

+

— 23 April —

George

Teacher's notes

Theme

This assembly is about standing up for what we believe is right.

Bible link

On that day, Leviathan, the sea monster, will squirm and try to escape, but the Lord will kill him with a cruel, sharp sword.
ISAIAH 27:1

In the Old Testament, God's victory over the sea monster Leviathan is sometimes used as a metaphor either for God's power over all creation or for his defeat of Israel's enemies. No one knows exactly what sort of monster Leviathan was, but the imagery is very much the same as that of the wriggling, twisting dragon defeated by St George. Traditionally, dragons represent monsters to be fought and subdued, as in the Old Testament picture of Leviathan.

The story of George's deeds of gallantry and his defeat of the dragon is first recorded in *The Golden Legend*, which was one of the most popular religious works of the Middle Ages. The work was compiled in 1275 by Jacobus de Voragine, a Dominican monk who became the Archbishop of Genoa.

Resources

A dragon (either picture or toy), princess and knight costumes, an English flag

Saint in context

George grew up in Lydda in Palestine around AD275–285. His parents were both from rich, noble families. After his parents died, George joined the Roman army and gained a reputation for daring deeds. He was tortured, then executed for his Christian faith after he refused to obey an order to worship pagan gods. The myth about his dragon-slaying grew up during the Crusades.

Entry point

Ask the children to think of people who are in the news because they have done what they think is right. Ask the children if they have ever had to stand up for what they believe is right. If appropriate, ask several children to share when and why they did this.

Reflection

George stood up for what he believed was right. Talk about ways we can stand up for what we believe is right. What would we do if we saw someone being bullied? What would we do if we saw someone stealing something or copying answers in a test?

Suggested songs

- When a knight won his spurs (*Come and Praise* 50)
- He who would valiant be (*Come and Praise* 44)
- The journey of life (*Come and Praise* 45)
- You may be happy (*Songs for Every Assembly*, Out of the Ark Music)

Optional prayer

Dear God, help us to know what we believe in and always to stand up for what is right.

'Build a saint' activity

Ask the children each to draw their own picture of a dragon and, on each scale, write or draw pictures of people or things that need to be fought against. This could be turned into a puzzle by writing words in which the vowels have been left out, so that other children have to work out what the words are: for example, gr--d, b-lly-ng, ch--t-ng, v-nd-l-sm or sw--r-ng. Place the children's pictures on the classroom display table as a symbol to remind the children of the story of St George.

The story retold

George lived in Israel nearly 300 years after Jesus' lifetime. The mighty Roman army was still strong and powerful and, as soon as he was old enough, George became a Roman soldier. He loved doing daring things and visiting new places.

On his travels, George heard about Jesus and decided to become a follower. Being a Christian helped George to be even more gallant. Then, one day in the year 303, the Roman Emperor, Diocletian, passed a law to say that no one was allowed to become a Christian. When George heard about this law, he took a deep breath. He had to make a choice. The first option was that he could remain in the Roman army, keep quiet about his faith and stop living as Jesus taught. The second was that he could leave the army and just keep quiet. The last was that he could try to do something about the law.

George chose the last option. Before he went to see the Roman Emperor, he gave away everything he owned. Deep down, he knew what was likely to happen to him: to ask the mighty Diocletian to change the law would lead to certain death.

On 23 April 304, George was killed because he had stood up for what he believed was right. His brave action has never been forgotten and the story has been passed down from parents to their children.

Nearly 1000 years later, during the Crusades, soldiers began creating stories about George. The story about how he killed the dragon and rescued the king's daughter grew up out of a book called *The Golden Legend*, which was written by the Archbishop of Genoa in about 1275.

In the story, a dragon made a nest by the water supply at Lydda, where George grew up. The dragon insisted that, if the people wanted water, they had to bring a sheep each day for him to eat. When all the sheep had been killed, a young girl was chosen by drawing lots. On the day the princess' name was drawn, George happened to be travelling through the town. He took on the dragon, fought it bravely and defended himself with his shield, which had the sign of the cross on it. George defeated the dragon, the princess was saved and the people decided to follow George's example and find out about the Christian faith.

George's symbol, a red cross on a white background, has become the design of the English flag. There is also a dragon in the middle of the Welsh flag.

Interactive retelling

Choose a child to play the role of St George and dress him or her up with sword, helmet and shield. Make sure that the volunteer is confident about being hot-seated and answering questions about the choices George had to make.

Story: George lives in Israel nearly 300 years after Jesus' lifetime. The mighty Roman army is still strong and powerful and, as soon as he is old enough, George becomes a Roman soldier. He loves doing daring things and visiting new places.

Interactive question: Which countries might George travel to, that are near Israel, and what daring deeds might a knight in shining armour have done at the end of the third century?

Story: On his travels, George hears about Jesus and decides to become a follower. Being a Christian helps George to be even more gallant. Then, one day in the year 303, the Roman Emperor, Diocletian, passes a law to say that no one is allowed to become a Christian. When George hears about this law, he takes a deep breath. He has to make a choice.

Interactive question: What options does George have?

Action: Hot-seat the child playing the role of George to find out how George feels about what has happened and what he is going to do next.

Story: The first option is that George can remain in the Roman army, keep quiet about his faith and stop living as Jesus taught. The second is that he can leave the army and just keep quiet. The last is that he can try to do something about the law.

George chooses the last option. Before he goes to see the Roman Emperor, he gives away everything he owns. Deep down, he knows what is likely to happen to him: to ask the mighty Diocletian to change the law will lead to certain death.

Interactive question: What would you have done?

Story: On 23 April 304, George is killed because he has stood up for what he believes is right. His brave action is never forgotten and the story is passed down from parents to their children.

Nearly 1000 years later, during the Crusades, soldiers begin creating stories about George. The story about how he killed the dragon and rescued the king's daughter grows up out of a book called *The Golden Legend*, written by the Archbishop of Genoa in about 1275.

Action: Choose children to act out the story as it unfolds.

Story: In the story, a dragon makes a nest by the water supply at Lydda, where George grew up. The dragon insists that, if the people want water, they have to bring a sheep each day for him to eat. When all the sheep have been killed, a young girl is chosen by drawing lots. On the day the princess' name is drawn, George happens to be travelling through the town. He takes on the dragon, fights it bravely and defends himself with his shield, which has the sign of the cross on it. George defeats the dragon, the princess is saved and the people decide to follow George's example and find out about the Christian faith.

George's symbol, a red cross on a white background, has become the design of the English flag. There is also a dragon in the middle of the Welsh flag.

+

— 25 April —

Mark

Teacher's notes

Theme

This assembly is about what is important in our lives.

Bible link

This is the good news about Jesus Christ, the Son of God.
MARK 1:1

Mark's Gospel is thought to have been the first account of Jesus' life that was written down. Many people think that Peter, one of Jesus' closest friends, helped Mark to write his account. Mark went on the first missionary journeys with Paul and Barnabas, telling people about Jesus. It is thought that he was killed for his faith when Nero was the emperor of Rome.

Resources

A scroll (made by attaching pieces of dowel to the top and bottom edges of a sheet of A4 paper and rolling the paper around the dowelling), some seeds, pictures of fishermen fishing

Saint in context

When Mark lived in Palestine, the Roman army occupied the country. Life was tough: people lived in fear, the climate was harsh, and life expectancy was low. Mark saw many of the things Jesus did, and heard many of the things he said. Mark also met with Jesus after the resurrection. In the early years of the Christian faith, Jesus' followers faced trouble from the religious authorities. Writing down the story of Jesus was just as dangerous as telling others about him, yet Mark bravely travelled with Paul, telling people about Jesus.

Entry point

Explore with the children how we find out what is happening in the world. Make a list of modern communication devices. Which is the children's favourite and why? How would they record something they wanted as many people as possible to read and find out about?

Reflection

Talk about how we record events in our lives. Perhaps we write things down in a diary or tell our families about what we do each day. Perhaps we have photographs to help us to remember when something important happens. What things would the children write down about their lives?

Suggested songs

- The Lord, the Lord (*Come and Praise* 108)
- Peace is flowing (*Come and Praise* 144)

Optional prayer

Dear God, thank you for people like Mark, who wrote details about Jesus' life so that we can find out more about him and what he did.

'Build a saint' activity

Place the scroll on the classroom display table to remind the children about the story of Mark. Have the children make their own scrolls by using two lollipop sticks and a sheet of A4 paper cut in half lengthways. On the scrolls, ask the children to write down something that happened recently that is important for other people to know about.

The story retold

Mark unrolled the scroll. The animal skin it was made from crinkled as he did so. In the flickering light, he and Peter moved closer so that they could read what had been written last time they were together.

'This is the good news about Jesus Christ, the Son of God,' the writing at the top of the scroll read.

So far, Mark had written about Jesus choosing the people he wanted to work closely with him. Peter had been one of the first. Peter was a fisherman and he had been mending his nets when Jesus walked by. There was something very special about Jesus, and Peter had known straight away that he wanted to take up Jesus' invitation to be one of his close friends.

Then Mark had written about Jesus healing people. There was a man with a skin disease, someone who couldn't walk, and others who couldn't see or hear and needed to be healed. Jesus helped them all.

Next, with Peter's help, Mark wrote down some of the stories Jesus had told. Jesus had a way of telling stories that helped people remember things and got them thinking. For example, there was the story about a mustard seed that grew into a huge bush. The meaning behind the story was plain to see: planting good things in people's hearts was like planting one little seed that grew and grew and grew until good things had spread far and wide.

Mark had also written about the time when Jesus had been sailing out on the lake with his friends. A storm had whipped up the waters and the disciples had been absolutely terrified. Then Jesus had stood up and told the wind and the waves to be quiet. Immediately, the storm had calmed right down. Then the disciples were frightened by what Jesus had done. No one else they knew could tell the rain and wind what to do.

Mark also wanted to write about what Jesus had said. Peter was able to tell him many things.

'Who do you say I am?' Jesus had asked.

'You are the Messiah!' Peter had replied straight away. He'd worked it out himself: he knew for certain that Jesus had been sent by God. At that time, Jesus had asked Peter not to tell anyone, but now things were different. People needed to know who Jesus was, which was one of the reasons Peter was helping Mark.

Tonight, Mark and Peter were going to record what happened in the last week of Jesus' life. Peter wanted so many things written down; so many little details. He had been there and wanted everything to be written exactly as it had happened.

Interactive retelling

Choose two children to play the roles of Mark and Peter and ask them to act out the story as it is told.

Story: Mark unrolls the scroll. The animal skin it is made from crinkles as he does so. In the flickering light, he and Peter move closer so that they can read what they wrote the last time they were together.

'This is the good news about Jesus Christ, the Son of God,' the writing at the top of the scroll reads.

Interactive question: What do you know about Jesus' life that might have been written on Mark's scroll?

Story: So far, Mark has written about Jesus choosing the people he wanted to work closely with him. Peter was one of the first. Peter is a fisherman and he was mending his nets when Jesus walked by. There was something very special about Jesus and Peter knew straight away that he wanted to take up Jesus' invitation to be one of his close friends.

Interactive question: Why might Peter have felt Jesus was special?

Story: Then Mark has written about Jesus healing people. There was a man with a skin disease, someone who couldn't walk, and others who couldn't see or hear and needed to be healed. Jesus helped them all.

Action: Act out the stories about Jesus healing people.

Story: Next, with Peter's help, Mark has written down some of the stories Jesus told. Jesus had a way of telling stories that helped people remember things and got them thinking. For example, there is the story about a mustard seed that grows into a huge bush. The meaning behind the story is plain to see: planting good things in people's hearts is like planting one little seed that grows and grows and grows until good things have spread far and wide.

Interactive question: How far have stories about Jesus spread today? How much have they grown?

Action: Ask the children to provide sound effects for the following story. They can make the noise of the rain by tapping their hands on their knees and the noise of the wind by making shushing noises. Encourage them to make the sound effects at the right levels, until everything is calm and quiet.

Story: Mark has also written about the time when Jesus was sailing out on the lake with his friends. A storm whipped up the waters and the disciples were absolutely terrified. Then Jesus stood up and told the wind and the waves to be quiet. Immediately, the storm calmed right down. Then the disciples were frightened by what Jesus had done. No one else they knew could tell the rain and wind what to do.

Interactive question: What five words would summarise the story of Jesus calming the storm?

Story: Mark also wanted to write about what Jesus said. Peter has been able to tell him many things.

'Who do you say I am?' Jesus once asked.

'You are the Messiah!' Peter replied straight away.

He had worked it out himself: he knew for certain that Jesus had been sent by God. At that time, Jesus asked Peter not to tell anyone, but now things are different. People need to know who Jesus is, which is one of the reasons Peter is helping Mark.

Interactive question: For what reasons might Jesus have asked Peter not to tell anyone when Peter realised that Jesus was the Son of God?

Story: Tonight, Mark and Peter are going to record what happened in the last week of Jesus' life. Peter wants so many things written down, so many little details. He was there and wants everything to be written exactly as it happened.

+

— 1 May —

Philip

Teacher's notes

Theme

This assembly is about asking questions.

Bible link

When Jesus saw the large crowd coming towards him, he asked Philip, 'Where will we get enough food to feed all these people?'
JOHN 6:5

Philip was one of Jesus' disciples. He saw Jesus perform miracles and heard him talk about God. He later became one of the first people to tell others about how Jesus had died, then risen from the dead. Philip asked Jesus lots of questions, but Jesus questioned Philip as well. One time this happened was when a large crowd gathered to listen to Jesus. Jesus already knew how he was going to make sure that everyone had enough to eat, but he asked Philip the question all the same so that he could hear what Philip's answer would be.

Resources

Five small rolls, a tin of sardines, simple costumes for those acting out the stories

Saint in context

Philip came from the town of Bethsaida on the shore of the Sea of Galilee. He was one of the first disciples whom Jesus invited to travel with him, so Philip saw at first hand what Jesus did and said. Traditionally, it is thought that Philip died for his faith at Hieropolis in Turkey about 50 years after Jesus' death and resurrection.

Entry point

Ask the children to share the best question they have ever come across. It could be a joke or a question that helped them understand something. What was the answer?

Reflection

Learning to ask questions is really important. Talk about whether there are any questions the children would like to know the answer to, and who they could ask to find out.

Suggested songs

- 5000+ hungry folk (*Kidsource* 2)
- Who took fish and bread? (*Junior Praise* 286)
- Thank you, Lord (*Come and Praise* 32)

Optional prayer

Dear God, sometimes it is difficult to understand things. Help us to ask the right questions and to persevere until we find the right answers.

'Build a saint' activity

Ask the children to draw a fish on a piece of paper and write down a question they would like to ask. On the back of the fish, they can write the name of someone who might be able to answer the question for them. Place the fish on the classroom display table as a reminder about the story of Philip.

The story retold

Philip came from Bethsaida on the shores of Lake Galilee—the same place that Nathaniel, Andrew and Peter were from. Philip was one of those people who always asked lots of questions, but he didn't always understand the answers he was given.

One day, a crowd of over 5000 people came to see Jesus. They spent the day listening to stories and watching people being healed. The afternoon was nearly over and the sun was beginning to sink in the sky when Jesus suddenly asked Philip where he could buy enough food to feed everyone.

'Don't you know that it would take almost a year's wages just to buy only a little bread for each of these people?' Philip replied. Philip probably wrinkled his face and wondered why Jesus had asked such a question. They were on a hill, miles away from the nearest village—and what baker could bake enough bread for 5000 people at short notice?

Then a little boy gave Jesus all the food he had—five barley loaves and two fish. It was not very much for 5000 people, but better than nothing. Jesus thanked the little boy and took the food. Then he thanked God and began to break the loaves into small pieces. The more he broke them, the more the bread kept on growing and growing and growing. It happened again with the fish. Suddenly, there was enough food for everyone.

The disciples asked the crowd to sit down and then they gave the food out. Everyone ate. Hungry tummies were filled. At the end of the meal, the disciples collected twelve basketfuls of bread and fish that had not been eaten.

Philip took part in Jesus' miracle. He saw what Jesus did,

he handed out the bread and he collected what was left after everyone had gone home. Yet still he didn't understand who Jesus was. Philip continually asked Jesus questions. It was the right thing to do—to keep asking questions until Philip understood the answer.

Interactive retelling

Choose four children to play the roles of Philip, Nathaniel, Andrew and Peter. Dress them in simple costumes.

Story: Philip comes from Bethsaida on the shores of Lake Galilee—the same place that Nathaniel, Andrew and Peter are from. Philip is one of those people who always asks lots of questions, but he doesn't always understand the answers he is given.

Interactive question: If you had been Philip, what questions would you want to ask Jesus?

Story: One day, a crowd of over 5000 people comes to see Jesus.

Action: Choose a further child to play the role of Jesus. Give him or her a simple costume to wear. Choose several other children to play the crowd of 5000.

Story: Everyone spends the day listening to stories and watching people being healed.

Action: Ask the children to act out Jesus talking and others listening, and some of the crowd being healed.

Story: The afternoon is nearly over and the sun is beginning to sink in the sky when Jesus suddenly asks Philip where he can buy enough food to feed everyone.

Interactive question: What might Philip's expression have been when he was asked the question… and why?

Story: 'Don't you know that it would take almost a year's wages just to buy only a little bread for each of these people?' Philip replies. Philip probably wrinkles his face and wonders why Jesus has asked such a question. They are on a hill, miles away from the nearest village—and what baker can bake enough bread for 5000 people at short notice?

Interactive question: What might Jesus' expression have been… and why?

Story: Then a little boy gives Jesus all the food he has—five barley loaves and two fish. It's not very much for 5000 people, but better than nothing. Jesus thanks the little boy and takes the food. Then he thanks God and begins to break the loaves into small pieces. The more he breaks them, the more the bread keeps on growing and growing and growing. It happens again with the fish. Suddenly, there is enough food for everyone.

The disciples ask the crowd to sit down and then they give the food out. Everyone eats. Hungry tummies are filled. At the end of the meal, the disciples collect twelve basketfuls of bread and fish that have not been eaten.

Interactive question: What questions might someone in the crowd have asked?

Action: Hot-seat members of the crowd. Ask the children what they thought about what Jesus did. Suggest that some people believed while others were still sceptical. Some might also have been frightened by what was happening.

Story: Philip takes part in Jesus' miracle. He sees what Jesus does, he hands out the bread and he collects what is left after everyone has gone home. Yet still he doesn't understand who Jesus is. Philip continually asks Jesus questions. It is the right thing to do—to keep asking questions until Philip understands the answer.

+

— 11 June —

Barnabas

Teacher's notes

Theme

This assembly is about life-changing events.

Bible link

'Go and preach the good news to everyone in the world.'
MARK 16:15

Two thousand years ago, Barnabas travelled with Paul, telling people about the new Christian faith and how it had changed their lives. They were obeying Jesus' instruction that they should take the message of Jesus' life, death and resurrection to everyone in the world.

Resources

Simple costumes for Paul and Barnabas

Saint in context

Barnabas grew up in Cyprus. It is not known when he became a Christian, but he appears very early in the story of the new Christian Church. After Paul had become a Christian and wanted to join the band of believers, it was Barnabas who helped everyone to understand that Paul's belief in Jesus was genuine and that he could be trusted. Traditionally, it is thought that Barnabas died for his faith at Salamis in Cyprus in AD61.

Entry point

Find out if the children know anyone who tells other people about their faith—for example, people who work for Christian charities such as the Trussell Trust, which is a charity based in Salisbury that provides food parcels for people in need in the UK. What do the people who work for charities such as this one do and why do they do it?

Reflection

Paul and Barnabas never knew what would happen when they told people about Jesus. In the town of Lystra, they healed a man who had been crippled all his life. Invite the children to try to imagine what the man might have felt like at the beginning of the day and how different he might have felt at the end of the day. He had been part of something that changed his life. Talk about times when we have been part of something that has changed our lives.

Suggested songs

- Love, joy, peace (*Light for Everyone* 10, SU)
- All the time (*Reach Up!* 11, SU)
- Peace, perfect peace (*Come and Praise* 53)
- Newspaper pictures (*Songs for Every Assembly*, Out of the Ark Music)

Optional prayer

Dear God, things happen sometimes that change our lives. Help us to remember that you are with us, whatever happens.

'Build a saint' activity

Ask the children to draw a picture of two people holding hands. Encourage them to think of a situation in which life changed after something happened. On one of the hands, invite them to write or draw what life was like before the change and, on the other hand, what it was like afterwards. Place the pictures on the classroom display table as a symbol to remind the children of the story of Barnabas. Talk about how their pictures can represent someone holding out a hand to help us when things in our lives suddenly change.

The story retold

Paul and Barnabas were both Christians in the early days of the church, who travelled together, telling people about Jesus. They visited many places, including the city of Lystra.

The day began well. The sun was shining and Paul and Barnabas went for a walk. As usual, they talked to people about their faith. A man who was sitting by the side of the road listened carefully to what they had to say. He couldn't walk, so the only way he could get enough money to buy food was to beg. After a while, Paul stopped talking and looked straight at the man. Everyone turned to look at the man, sensing that something was about to happen.

'Stand up!' Paul suddenly said.

There was silence. Was he really expecting a crippled man to get up? Did God heal people? Was a miracle about to take place?

The man jumped up and started walking round.

'Thank you, God!' Barnabas whispered as he saw the man leaping and dancing with joy.

Everyone stared at Paul and Barnabas. Everyone cheered. Then things started getting out of hand.

'They are gods!' someone shouted. 'The gods have turned into humans!'

Before they realised what was happening, Paul and Barnabas were being given flowers and named as Zeus and Hermes, who were gods that the ancient Greeks worshipped. Barnabas and Paul ripped open their clothes to show that they were made of skin and bones.

'We are humans just like you. We are not gods!' they shouted back. 'We have just come to tell you about Jesus.'

Paul and Barnabas could never predict what would happen when they told people about Jesus, but being mistaken for Greek gods was not what they had planned.

When the crowd realised their mistake, they became so angry that they began hurling stones. The situation got so bad that the people thought they had killed Paul. They dragged him out of the city and left him for dead.

Thankfully, Paul survived. By the next day, he had recovered and was ready to carry on his journey with Barnabas. The Bible does not say what happened to the man who was healed. It would be interesting to know what he thought about it all, because his life had been completely changed for ever.

Interactive retelling

Choose two children to play the roles of Paul and Barnabas and act out the story as it unfolds. Give them simple costumes to wear.

Story: Paul and Barnabas are both Christians in the early days of the Church, who travel together, telling people about Jesus. They visit many places, including the city of Lystra.

The day begins well. The sun is shining and Paul and Barnabas go for a walk. As usual, they talk to people about their faith.

Action: Choose a child to play the role of the man sitting by the roadside, and others to be the crowd. They act out the story as it unfolds.

Story: A man who is sitting by the side of the road listens carefully to what Paul and Barnabas have to say. He can't walk, so the only way he can get enough money to buy food is to beg. After a while, Paul stops talking and looks straight at the man. Everyone turns to look at the man, sensing something is about to happen.

Interactive question: What different thoughts might people be thinking?

Story: 'Stand up!' Paul suddenly says.

There is silence. Is he really expecting a man who can't walk to get up? Does God heal people? Is a miracle about to take place?

The man jumps up and starts walking round.

'Thank you, God!' Barnabas whispers as he sees the man leaping and dancing with joy.

Interactive question: What will the greatest change be for the man?

Story: Everyone stares at Paul and Barnabas. Everyone cheers. Then things start getting out of hand.

'They are gods!' someone shouts. 'The gods have turned into humans!'

Before they realise what is happening, Paul and Barnabas are being given flowers and named as Zeus and Hermes, who are gods that the ancient Greeks worship. Barnabas and Paul rip their clothes open to show that they are made of skin and bones.

'We are humans just like you. We are not gods!' they shout back. 'We have just come to tell you about Jesus.'

Interactive question: What would you have done if you had been Paul or Barnabas?

Story: Paul and Barnabas can never predict what will happen when they tell people about Jesus, but being mistaken for Greek gods is not what they have planned.

When the crowd realise their mistake, they become so angry that they begin hurling stones. The situation gets so bad that the people think they have killed Paul. They drag him out of the city and leave him for dead.

Thankfully, Paul survives. By the next day, he has recovered and is ready to carry on his journey with Barnabas. The Bible does not say what happened to the man who was healed. It would be interesting to know what he thinks about it all, because his life has been completely changed for ever.

+

— 29 June —

Peter

Teacher's notes

Theme

This assembly is about thinking before we speak.

Bible link

When Jesus was alone praying, his disciples came to him, and he asked them, 'What do people say about me?' They answered, 'Some say that you are John the Baptist or Elijah or a prophet from long ago who has come back to life. Then Jesus asked them, 'But who do you say I am?' Peter answered, 'You are the Messiah sent from God.'

LUKE 9:18–20

Peter was one of Jesus' close friends and followers. He is recorded as being one of the first people to recognise that Jesus was the Messiah—the person God had promised to send to teach the truth about God. Peter was also the person who denied he even knew Jesus after Jesus was arrested (Matthew 26:69–75).

Resources

Newspaper articles that report something someone has said about someone else; items to represent fishing nets, boats, coins and a rock; simple costumes for Peter, Andrew and Jesus

Saint in context

Peter was a fisherman who lived under Roman occupation in Galilee at the time of Jesus. He worked with his brother, Andrew. Peter was known as Simon until Jesus changed his name to Peter, which means 'a rock'. Jesus said that he would build his church on Peter, the rock. Peter denied he knew Jesus after Jesus was arrested, but Jesus forgave him over a breakfast on the beach after the resurrection. Peter went on to be one of the founding members of the Christian Church. Traditionally, it is thought he was killed for his faith in Rome in AD64.

Entry point

Read out some newspaper stories that report something someone has said about someone else. Ask the children to think about how the things that have been said might change one person's attitude towards another.

Reflection

Sometimes Peter said things that he had thought hard about. At other times he seemed to speak without thinking. Talk about times when we say something we have thought hard about. Think of other times when we say something that we later wish we hadn't said. How does each of these times make us feel inside? How do our words affect other people?

Suggested songs

- A stranger walked along the shore (*Kidsource* 410)
- When Jesus walked in Galilee (*Come and Praise* 25)

Optional prayer

Dear God, thank you that you know us so well and forgive us when we get things wrong. Help us to think before we speak and not to say things that are untrue or hurtful to other people.

'Build a saint' activity

Add a rock to the classroom display table as a symbol to remind the children about the story of Peter. If the rock has both jagged and smooth parts, ask the children which is a better symbol for Peter, the rough part or the smooth part. On speech bubbles, write some of the things Peter is known to have said. Which speech bubbles belong on the jagged part of the rock? Which belong on the smooth part?

The story retold

Another day lay ahead. Simon sighed. All he ever seemed to do was fish. He and his brother would go out in the boats and drop their nets. When the nets were full of teeming fish, they'd row back to the shore and drag the heaving nets on to the beach. Then they'd have to visit the tax man. For every fish they caught, they had to pay money to the Roman government.

But this day was different. This day had something in it that would change Simon's life for ever. Today, as Simon and Andrew mended their nets in the hot sunshine, a man walked along the beach towards them. They heard him coming, looked up and saw his face. He stopped and chatted. There was something very special about him. Simon and Andrew both stood up. They left their nets and followed the teacher. For the time being, their nets could wait.

The more Simon and Andrew stayed with Jesus, the more they learned who he really was. They saw what he did and how he helped people. They heard him tell amazing stories.

One day, Jesus turned to his friends and asked, 'Who do you think I am?' Simon thought for a little while, then he answered, 'You are the Messiah sent from God.' Simon knew that this teacher who had become his friend was very special.

Jesus changed Simon's name to Peter, which meant 'rock'.

'I will never leave you, even if the rest do!' Peter promised Jesus. Jesus stared at Peter.

'You will say three times that you do not know me,' Jesus whispered.

'I will never say that, even if I have to die with you!' Peter gasped. Jesus' words seemed so harsh, but Peter didn't know himself as well as Jesus knew him. Just before Jesus died, Peter did exactly what Jesus had said. He let Jesus down when it really mattered. Peter thought about it a lot afterwards. If only he hadn't said those words!

Jesus knew how awful Peter felt. One day, after Jesus had died and come back to life, he spent time with Peter, helping him to know that he was forgiven. Peter went on to be one of the first people to start building the Christian Church.

Interactive retelling

Choose children to play the roles of Simon Peter, Andrew and Jesus. Dress them in simple costumes and ask them to act out the story as it unfolds.

Story: Another day lies ahead. Simon sighs. All he ever seems to do is fish. He and his brother go out in the boats and drop their nets. When the nets are full of teeming fish, they row back to the shore and drag the heaving nets on to the beach. Then they have to visit the tax man. For every fish they catch, they have to pay money to the Roman government.

Interactive questions: What might Simon Peter like best about his job? What might he not like about it?

Story: But this day is different. This day has something in it that will change Simon's life for ever. Today, as Simon and Andrew mend their nets in the hot sunshine, a man walks along the beach towards them. They hear him coming, look up and see his face. He stops and chats. There is something very special about him. Simon and Andrew both stand up. They leave their nets and follow the teacher. For the time being, their nets can wait.

The more Simon and Andrew stay with Jesus, the more they learn who he really is. They see what he does and how he helps people. They hear him tell amazing stories.

Interactive question: What stories might Peter have heard Jesus tell?

Story: One day Jesus turns to his friends and asks, 'Who do you think I am?' Simon thinks for a little while, then he answers, 'You are the Messiah sent from God.' Simon knows that this teacher who has become his friend is very special.

Interactive question: What miracles might Peter have seen, to make him think that Jesus has come from God?

Story: Jesus changes Simon's name to Peter, which means 'a rock'.

'I will never leave you, even if the rest do!' Peter promises Jesus. Jesus stares at Peter.

'You will say three times that you do not know me,' Jesus whispers.

'I will never say that, even if I have to die with you!' Peter gasps. Jesus' words seem so harsh, but Peter doesn't know himself as well as Jesus knows him. Just before Jesus dies, Peter does exactly what Jesus has said. He lets Jesus down when it really matters. Peter thinks about it a lot afterwards. If only he hadn't said those words!

Interactive question: How does Peter feel when he knows he has let his friend down so badly by what he has said?

Story: Jesus knows how awful Peter feels. One day, after Jesus has died and come back to life, he spends time with Peter, helping him to know that he is forgiven. Peter goes on to be one of the first people to start building the Christian Church.

+

— 3 July —

Thomas

Teacher's notes

Theme

This assembly is about wondering about the truth.

Bible link

Thomas said, 'First, I must see the nail scars in his hands and touch them with my finger. I must put my hand where the spear went into his side. I won't believe unless I do this!'
JOHN 20:25

Thomas was one of the people Jesus chose to be a close disciple. Whenever we meet him in the Gospel stories, Thomas comes across as a straightforward person who wants things explained fully before he will accept them. Thomas wasn't with the other disciples when Jesus first appeared to them after the resurrection, and when he heard their story he refused to believe the report that Jesus was alive. A week later, upon meeting Jesus himself, he readily changed his mind and confessed Jesus to be his Lord and his God.

Resources

Simple costumes for Jesus, Thomas, Mary, Peter, John and two other disciples; chairs for the disciples to sit on

Saint in context

Thomas' name means 'twin' in Aramaic. Along with the other disciples, he spent much time with Jesus. Thomas could be blunt and pessimistic in his approach to what he saw and heard. He was the disciple who thought that going with Jesus would eventually lead to his own death, yet he was still prepared to go (John 11:16) and, when Jesus reminded his disciples that they knew where he was going when he returned to heaven, Thomas bluntly told Jesus that they actually did not know (John 14:1–5). After the resurrection, Thomas is the one who refuses to believe that Jesus has risen from the dead, but he is also the first to say of Jesus, 'You are my Lord and my God' when eventually he sees the truth. Later, Thomas travelled outside the Roman Empire to tell others about Jesus.

Entry point

Ask the children to think of questions they might be asked during the day ahead. Invite several children to the front to share their answers. Next, ask a child to come to the front and put the questions in order of long-term importance. For example, 'Why does your heart beat faster when you take exercise?' is more important than 'What have you got for lunch today?'

Reflection

Thomas was someone who always wanted to get to the bottom of what he saw and heard. He wanted to know the truth. Sometimes we can jump to conclusions, but it is always best to take time to work out the answers. Encourage the children to think about the most important question they have ever wondered about and to think of someone they could go to for the answer.

Suggested songs

- Jesus in the garden (*Come and Praise* 129)
- One more step along the world I go (*Come and Praise* 47)
- Sun and moon in the starlit sky (*Songs for Every Assembly*, Out of the Ark Music)

Optional prayer

Dear God, give us courage to ask difficult questions and to keep on asking until we find the answers.

'Build a saint' activity

Ask the children to draw a big question mark in bubble writing. Inside it, ask them to write questions that are important to ask and find answers to. Add the question marks to the classroom display table as a symbol to remind the children of the story of Thomas.

The story retold

Thomas didn't go too close in case someone saw him and tried to arrest him, too, but by the end of that first Good Friday, he knew that Jesus had died. There was no doubt whatsoever in his mind. The Roman soldiers had made sure that Jesus was dead. Those were the facts. He had to accept them.

Thomas joined the other disciples and, together, they hid themselves away. They were so scared that what had happened to Jesus would also happen to them. Some of the women had ventured out. Jesus' friend, Mary, was one of those who did. She had gone to Jesus' tomb, and there something extraordinary had happened. Through her tears of sorrow, Mary had turned to see Jesus standing next to her. He had spoken to her, called her name, and reassured her. Trembling with fear and excitement, she had run back to tell the others her news. Peter and John had then also headed off to the tomb where Jesus' body had been laid. When they came back, they said that the tomb was empty. Only the strips of cloth that Jesus' body had been wrapped in were still there.

It was all nonsense, of course, thought Thomas. No one comes back from the dead. Thomas went out. He wanted to be by himself to get his head straight and to think, but when he went back in the room the madness started all over again. Everyone was saying that Jesus had come into the room and spoken to them.

'We have seen the Lord!' they told him. It was beyond a joke.

Thomas looked at them. Of course he did not believe them.

'First, I must see the nail scars in his hands and touch them with my finger. I must put my hand where the spear went into his side. I won't believe unless I do this!' he said.

He wasn't rude. He just said it very firmly. But his friends kept on about it—for a whole week. The joke was wearing very thin, and it hadn't been very funny in the first place. Then it happened. Thomas was with everyone else this time.

Jesus came in while the doors were still locked and stood in the middle of the group. He greeted the disciples. Thomas knew that voice.

'Put your finger here and look at my hands! Put your hand into my side. Stop doubting and have faith!'

Thomas' mouth dropped open. His chest tightened. It wasn't a joke. Jesus was really here. He had come back to life.

The others had been right. Jesus even knew what Thomas had said. Thomas felt awful about that. Even worse, Jesus probably also knew what he had thought. He looked at Jesus and their eyes met. Thomas would never forget that moment.

'My Lord and my God!' he gasped. Thomas was the first disciple to say those words to Jesus. The word 'Lord' means 'master' and the word 'God' means someone who is worshipped and loved. That was how Thomas saw Jesus. Jesus had answered Thomas' questions and cleared all doubt from his mind.

Interactive retelling

Choose children to play the roles of Thomas, Mary, Peter and John. Give them simple costumes to wear and ask them to sit on chairs at one side of the room. Place a chair at the other side of the room to represent the tomb. Choose another child to play the role of Jesus and ask him or her to stand near the chair representing the tomb. Ask all the characters to act out the story as it unfolds.

Story: Thomas doesn't go too close in case someone sees him and tries to arrest him, too, but by the end of that first Good Friday, he knows that Jesus has died. There is no doubt whatsoever in his mind. The Roman soldiers have made sure that Jesus is dead. Those are the facts. He has to accept them.

Thomas joins the other disciples and, together, they hide themselves away. They are so scared that what has happened to Jesus will also happen to them. Some of the women venture out. Jesus' friend, Mary, is one of them.

Action: Mary walks across the room to where the tomb is.

Story: Mary goes to Jesus' tomb, and there something extraordinary happens. Through her tears of sorrow, Mary turns to see Jesus standing next to her. He speaks to her, calls her name, and reassures her. Trembling with fear and excitement, she runs back to tell the others her news.

Action: Jesus and Mary mime their meeting and then Mary runs back to the disciples. Jesus stands back so that he is no longer near the tomb.

Story: Peter and John then also head off to the tomb where Jesus' body is laid.

Action: Peter and John run across the room to where the tomb is.

Story: When they come back, they say that the tomb is empty. Only the strips of cloth that Jesus' body was wrapped in are still there.

Interactive question: How might you have reacted to the news if you had been one of the disciples?

Story: It is all nonsense, of course, thinks Thomas. No one comes back from the dead. Thomas goes out. He wants to be by himself to get his head straight and to think, but when he comes back in the room the madness has started all over again. Everyone is saying that Jesus has come into the room and spoken to them.

'We have seen the Lord!' they tell him. It is beyond a joke.

Interactive question: What might you feel if you were Thomas at this point in the story?

Story: Thomas looks at them. Of course he doesn't believe them.

Action: Ask Thomas to read the lines below.

Thomas: First, I must see the nail scars in his hands and touch them with my finger. I must put my hand where the spear went into his side. I won't believe unless I do this!

Story: Thomas isn't rude. He just says it very firmly. But his friends keep on about it—for a whole week. The joke is wearing very thin, and it wasn't very funny in the first place. Then it happens. Thomas is with everyone else this time.

Jesus comes in while the doors are still locked and stands in the middle of the group. He greets the disciples. Thomas knows that voice.

Action: Jesus walks across the room and stands in the middle of the group. He or she reads the words below.

Jesus: Put your finger here and look at my hands! Put your hand into my side. Stop doubting and have faith!

Interactive question: How might Thomas feel now?

Story: Thomas' mouth drops open. His chest tightens. It isn't a joke. Jesus is really here. He has come back to life. The others were right. Jesus even knows what Thomas has said. Thomas feels awful about that. Even worse, Jesus probably also knows what he has thought. He looks at Jesus and their eyes meet. Thomas will never forget that moment.

'My Lord and my God!' he gasps. Thomas is the first disciple to say those words to Jesus. The word 'Lord' means 'master' and the word 'God' means someone who is worshipped and loved. That is how Thomas sees Jesus. Jesus has answered Thomas' questions and cleared all doubt from his mind.

+

— 22 July —

Mary Magdalene

Teacher's notes

Theme

This assembly is about the Easter story.

Bible link

Mary Magdalene stood crying outside the tomb.
JOHN 20:11

Mary Magdalene was one of several women from Galilee who travelled with Jesus as he went from place to place, teaching people about God. Mary was also present when Jesus died on the cross. On the first Easter morning, Mary had gone to the tomb with special ointments to anoint Jesus' body—but she found that the tomb was empty.

Resources

Find pictures of the Easter story to illustrate the text. If possible, enlarge and project them on to a screen

Saint in context

Mary was a follower of Jesus. Traditionally, she is believed to have been the person who poured expensive perfume over Jesus' feet. Her actions, which showed how much she loved Jesus, enraged some of those present who thought that the perfume could have been sold and the money given to people in need. Mary was the person who ran to fetch Peter and John after she had found the tomb empty. After they left, she was the first person to meet Jesus after he rose from death.

Entry point

Explore the symbolic reasons why chocolate eggs and hot cross buns are eaten at Easter time. Why would Jesus not have eaten them? Find out what the children know about the Easter story.

Reflection

For Christians, Easter is not really about chocolate and hot cross buns—although Christians do enjoy eating them. Talk about what Christians celebrate at Easter time (the time when Jesus died, then came back to life again). Christians believe that Jesus was God's Son and that he died so that everyone could be friends with God.

Suggested songs

- When Jesus walked in Galilee (*Come and Praise* 25)
- Jesus in the garden (*Come and Praise* 129)
- All in an Easter garden (*Come and Praise* 130)
- Now the green blade rises (*Come and Praise* 131)
- Sing out an Easter song (*Kidsource* 701)

Optional prayer

Dear God, as we enjoy Easter foods, help us to remember that Christians believe Jesus died and came back to life again.

'Build a saint' activity

Ask the children to draw a picture of an Easter garden with the empty tomb. Alternatively, make simple Easter gardens using paper plates as the base, cardboard egg trays for the tomb and moss for the garden. Place the Easter garden pictures or models on the classroom display table as a symbol to remind the children about the story of Mary. Draw pictures of the events that happened during Easter week and place them among the Easter gardens.

The story retold

Mary stood on the hillside, watching Jesus die. He'd never hurt anyone; he'd helped and healed so many people. Yet here he was, nailed to a wooden cross, gasping for breath, being killed by brutal, cruel soldiers who were laughing and chatting as they watched him die. She could hear them and yet she could do nothing about it.

Jesus was the most important person in Mary's life. He had rescued her from many things that had hurt her. From the day of their very first meeting, she had travelled with him, looking after his needs and watching and listening to all he did and said. Mary believed that Jesus was the Messiah, the holy one sent from God. How could it come to this? She wiped her tears away with the back of her hand.

Three days passed. They were sad days for Mary, with nothing but an empty aching inside, as she kept wondering why Jesus had died. She was fearful about what would happen next. On the morning of the third day—the Sunday morning—Mary went to the garden where Jesus' dead body had been laid inside a tomb. She wanted to anoint him with special perfumed oil as a final parting gift.

But the tomb was empty. The body had gone. Mary looked around her. Was it thieves who had broken into the tomb? That did happen sometimes. People stole the strips of cloth that dead bodies were wrapped in. They were that desperate.

There was someone there with her now. She looked up. It was just the gardener.

'Why are you crying?' he asked her. Mary burst into fresh tears as she tried to explain her fears about robbers. 'They have taken away my Lord's body!' she cried. 'I don't know where they have taken him.'

'Who is it you're looking for?' he asked again.

'Sir, if you have taken his body away, please tell me so that I can go and get him,' Mary stammered through her tears. There was silence. Then the man said just one word to her.

'Mary.'

Mary froze. She suddenly recognised his voice. Slowly, she turned towards him. The pain inside her melted away. It was him! It was Jesus!

'Rabboni!' she gasped. The word meant teacher and master.

Her teacher and her Lord had risen from the dead!

Interactive retelling

Story: Mary stands on the hillside, watching Jesus die. He's never hurt anyone; he's helped and healed so many people. Yet here he is, nailed to a wooden cross, gasping for breath, being killed by brutal, cruel soldiers who are laughing and chatting as they watch him die. She can hear them and yet she can do nothing about it.

Interactive question: What do the children already know about this part of the Easter story?

Story: Jesus is the most important person in Mary's life. He has rescued her from many things that have hurt her. From the day of their very first meeting, she has travelled with him, looking after his needs and watching and listening to all he has done and said. Mary believes that Jesus is the Messiah, the holy one sent from God. How could it have come to this? She wipes her tears away with the back of her hand.

Interactive question: Another word for 'Messiah' is 'Christ'. What do Christians believe about Jesus that makes them give him the name 'Jesus Christ'?

Story: Three days pass. They are sad days for Mary, with nothing but an empty aching inside, as she keeps wondering why Jesus has died. She is fearful of what will happen next. On the morning of the third day—the Sunday morning—Mary goes to the garden where Jesus' dead body has been laid inside a tomb. She wants to anoint him with special perfumed oil as a final parting gift.

Interactive question: What other story do we know about someone bringing the gift of a special perfumed oil to Jesus? (The wise men brought frankincense and myrrh to Jesus when he was born.)

Story: But the tomb is empty. The body has gone. Mary looks around her. Is it thieves who have broken into the tomb? That does happen sometimes. People steal the strips of cloth that dead bodies are wrapped in. They are that desperate. There is someone there with her now. She looks up. It is just the gardener.

'Why are you crying?' he asks her. Mary bursts into fresh tears as she tries to explain her fears about robbers. 'They have taken away my Lord's body!' she cries. 'I don't know where they have taken him.'

'Who is it you're looking for?' he asks again.

'Sir, if you have taken his body away, please tell me so that I can go and get him,' Mary stammers through her tears. There is silence. Then the man says just one word to her.

Interactive question: If you were Mary, which word would you want Jesus to say?

Story: 'Mary.'

Mary freezes. She suddenly recognises his voice. Slowly, she turns towards him. The pain inside her melts away. It is him! It is Jesus!

'Rabboni!' she gasps. The word means teacher and master.

Her teacher and her Lord has risen from the dead!

+

— 25 July —

James

Theme

This assembly is about when unexpected things happen.

Bible link

Jesus walked on and soon saw James and John, the sons of Zebedee. They were in a boat, mending their nets. At once Jesus asked them to come with him. They left their father in the boat with the hired workers and went with him.

MARK 1:19–20

James was the brother of John, who was the author of John's Gospel. The two brothers were both chosen by Jesus to be among his twelve closest disciples.

Life with Jesus must have been unpredictable. They moved round the country with their teacher, listening to what he said and watching him perform miracles. There were some occasions when Jesus asked just a few of his close friends to be with him: he chose Peter, James and his brother, John. One such occasion was when Jesus brought a child back from the dead. In his Gospel, Mark tells us that Jesus' words to the girl were simply, 'Little girl, get up!'

Resources

Simple costumes for the children playing the roles of Jesus, Peter, James and John, Jairus and his wife and daughter

Saint in context

Peter and his brother, Andrew, and James and his brother, John, were the first people that Jesus chose to be his closest disciples. All four were fishermen, living and working on the shores of Lake Galilee. James and John were the sons of Zebedee. They left their father in his boat with the hired hands when Jesus asked them to go with him. The two brothers are thought to have had tempestuous temperaments. Jesus even described them as 'thunderbolts' (Mark 3:17). After Jesus' death and resurrection, James continued to tell others about the new faith. He was martyred in AD44 by Herod Agrippa.

Entry point

Ask the children to share things that have happened to them that they did not expect to happen.

Reflection

James had to learn to cope with the unexpected. Talk about how we cope when something happens to us that we didn't know was going to happen. What does it feel like? Are there any experiences the children would like to talk about? Was their experience good or bad? Do they still think about it now?

Suggested songs

- Lay my white cloak on the ground (*Come and Praise* 112)
- Light up the fire (*Come and Praise* 55)

Optional prayer

Dear God, when unexpected things happen to us, help us to cope and to remain as calm and sensible as possible. Thank you that you were there to help Jairus' family and that you are also here to help us today.

'Build a saint' activity

Make a drawing of a little girl or model the figure out of clay or playdough. If possible, design her so that she can lie down, then sit up. Add the models to the classroom display table to remind the children about the story of James and Jairus' daughter.

The story retold

'My little daughter is very ill. Please come and make her better,' the man begged.

'Looks like we'll be on the move again,' James thought. Being with Jesus, he never quite knew what was going to happen next, or where he would be at the end of each day. He and his brother, John, loved the excitement of their life with Jesus. It was so much better than catching and selling fish all the time, which was what they used to do as fishermen living on the shores of Lake Galilee.

Just as James had predicted, Jesus set off for the man's house. The man, whose name was Jairus, was in charge of the Jewish meeting place in the town, so he was quite an important person. As Jesus and his disciples followed Jairus, many of the people tagged along, too, pushing and jostling as they crowded around Jesus. Their progress was slow, with lots of distractions.

Suddenly, some men pushed through the crowd. They were looking for Jairus and called out his name until they found him.

'Your daughter has died,' they said.

Jairus' face crumpled. He felt completely helpless. There was nothing that could be done. His daughter was dead. But

Jesus had overheard the men. 'Don't worry,' he said to Jairus. 'Just have faith!' Jesus often said unexpected things!

Taking Peter, James and John with him, Jesus quickly set off for Jairus' house. When they arrived, they had to squeeze through a crowd of people who were weeping and wailing. Jesus said to them, 'Why are you crying and carrying on like this? The child isn't dead. She is just asleep.'

The people laughed at him, but Jesus sent them all away. He took Peter, James and John into the house with Jairus and his wife. They went to where the child was lying. James could see that the men had been right—the poor little girl had died. He felt so sorry for her, lying there with her little white face and no breath in her body. She was only twelve years old. But Jesus smiled gently and took her by the hand. James' eyes widened. Was Jesus going to...? Surely he couldn't bring her back from the dead!

'Little girl, get up!'

The little girl stirred. Her eyes flickered open. She got straight up and started to walk around!

'He's brought her back to life!' someone gasped. Everyone was greatly surprised—including James, Peter and John (who should have known better).

Jesus wasn't surprised. 'Give her something to eat,' he said calmly. Being dead must have made the little girl very hungry!

Interactive retelling

If desired, the story can be told using children to act out the parts of the different characters. Alternatively, the interactive questions can be used on their own to help the children to understand the story better.

Story: 'My little daughter is very ill. Please come and make her better,' the man begs.

'Looks like we'll be on the move again,' James thinks. Being with Jesus, he never quite knows what is going to happen next, or where he will be at the end of each day. He and his brother, John, love the excitement of their life with Jesus. It's so much better than catching and selling fish all the time, which is what they used to do as fishermen living on the shores of Lake Galilee.

Interactive question: What unusual things might James see as he travels with Jesus?

Story: Just as James has predicted, Jesus sets off for the man's house. The man, whose name is Jairus, is in charge of the Jewish meeting place in the town, so he is quite an important person.

Interactive question: What other jobs did people do in Jesus' day?

Story: As Jesus and his disciples follow Jairus, many of the people tag along, too, pushing and jostling as they crowd around Jesus. Their progress is slow, with lots of distractions.

Suddenly, some men push through the crowd. They are looking for Jairus and call out his name until they find him.

'Your daughter has died,' they say.

Jairus' face crumples. He feels completely helpless. There is nothing that can be done. His daughter is dead.

Interactive question: How might you have felt if you had been Jairus?

Story: But Jesus overhears the men. 'Don't worry,' he says to Jairus. 'Just have faith!' Jesus often says unexpected things!

Taking Peter, James and John with him, Jesus quickly sets off for Jairus' house. When they arrive, they have to squeeze through a crowd of people who are weeping and wailing. Jesus says to them, 'Why are you crying and carrying on like this? The child isn't dead. She is just asleep.'

Interactive question: What do you think the crowd thinks of Jesus?

Story: The people laugh at him, but Jesus sends them all away. He takes Peter, James and John into the house with Jairus and his wife. They go to where the child is lying. James can see that the men were right—the poor little girl has died. He feels so sorry for her, lying there with her little white face and no breath in her body. She is only twelve years old. But Jesus smiles gently and takes her by the hand. James' eyes widen. Is Jesus going to…? Surely he can't bring her back from the dead!

'Little girl, get up!'

The little girl stirs. Her eyes flicker open. She gets straight up and starts to walk around!

'He's brought her back to life!' someone gasps. Everyone is greatly surprised—including James, Peter and John (who should have known better).

Jesus isn't surprised. 'Give her something to eat,' he says calmly. Being dead must have made the little girl very hungry!

Also by Heather Butler

35 Stories to Make You Think

Teaching values through RE

35 Stories to Make You Think is a compilation of the popular 'Stories to Make You Think' series, addressing a range of topical and often sensitive issues relevant to the lives of children in Years 3–6. It can be used on a one-to-one basis in a group, or with a whole class during Circle Time, PSHE, Citizenship or Religious Education. The 35 issues are covered under four distinct headings: 'Family life', 'Life and death', 'Community life' and 'Personal life'.

Each chapter follows the same format and includes:

- Story summary
- RE concept
- Exploring the concept
- Key Bible verse
- Bible story link
- Story time
- Things children have said
- Thinking time for children
- Optional prayer

ISBN 978 184101 506 4 £9.99
Available direct from BRF using the order form on page 175. You may also order at www.brfonline.org.uk.

Also from BRF/Barnabas

Stories of Everyday Saints

40 stories with Bible links and related activities

Veronica Heley

The 40 men and women whose stories are told in this book were used by God to do his work. Saints are people who listen to God and try to do what he wants.

Some of the people covered have been formally named as saints by their church. In such cases, their name appears with 'St' before it, as in 'St Patrick'. Others have not been recognised publicly in this way but are included in the book because God used them to carry out a particular task. These people are referred to simply by their ordinary names, such as 'Florence Nightingale'.

The saints in this book fall into four categories:

- Bible saints from the New Testament, such as St Paul
- Historical and legendary saints, such as St George
- Worldwide saints, such as St Francis of Assisi
- More recent and contemporary saints, such as Mother Teresa

Each story is accompanied by a key date and brief description of the saint, a Bible link and prayer, related activities and suggested songs.

ISBN 978 184101 224 7 £9.99
Available direct from BRF using the order form on page 175. You may also order at www.brfonline.org.uk.

Also from BRF/Barnabas

Story Assemblies for the School Year

36 assemblies with five-minute stories, teacher's notes and RE follow-up

Edward J. Carter

This book is full of memorable parables about God and biblical events, creatively told to engage and delight pupils at primary level.

There are six themes in total, each with its own easy-to-make storytelling prop. The stories within each theme are divided into six weekly episodes, covering a wide range of contemporary values and topics for the whole school year. The six themes are:

- God's creation
- The message of the Old Testament prophets
- Stories about Christian values
- The story of Holy Week and Easter
- Jesus' resurrection and ascension
- The journeys of the apostle Paul

As well as being ideal for collective worship, there are practical follow-up ideas to help children connect with the stories in the classroom.

ISBN 978 184101 699 3 £8.99
Available direct from BRF using the order form on page 175. You may also order at www.brfonline.org.uk.

ORDERFORM

REF	TITLE	PRICE	QTY	TOTAL
506 4	35 Stories to Make You Think	£9.99		
224 7	Stories of Everyday Saints	£9.99		
699 3	Story Assemblies for the School Year	£8.99		
		Postage and packing		
		Donation		
		TOTAL		

POSTAGE AND PACKING CHARGES

Order value	UK	Europe	Surface	Air Mail
£7.00 & under	£1.25	£3.00	£3.50	£5.50
£7.10–£30.00	£2.25	£5.50	£6.50	£10.00
Over £30.00	FREE	prices on request		

Name ______________________ Account Number __________

Address ______________________________________

______________________ Postcode __________

Telephone Number ______________________

Email ______________________________________

Payment by: ❑ Cheque ❑ Mastercard ❑ Visa ❑ Postal Order ❑ Maestro

Card no ☐☐☐☐ ☐☐☐☐ ☐☐☐☐ ☐☐☐☐ ☐☐☐

Valid from ☐☐☐☐ Expires ☐☐☐☐ Issue no. ☐☐☐

Security code* ☐☐☐ *Last 3 digits on the reverse of the card. ESSENTIAL IN ORDER TO PROCESS YOUR ORDER

Shaded boxes for Maestro use only

Signature ______________________ Date __________

All orders must be accompanied by the appropriate payment.

Please send your completed order form to:

BRF, 15 The Chambers, Vineyard, Abingdon OX14 3FE
Tel. 01865 319700 / Fax. 01865 319701 Email: enquiries@brf.org.uk

❑ Please send me further information about BRF publications.

Available from your local Christian bookshop.

BRF is a Registered Charity